Essays on
Shakespeare and
European Renaissance Culture
(1874 & 1876)

Wilhelm König

Essays on Shakespeare and European Renaissance Culture (1874 & 1876)

Translated by Ritchie Robertson

Edited and with a Preface by Elisabetta Tarantino

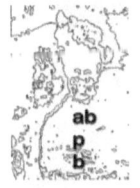

Abingdon, UK
2024

Original: 'Ueber die Entlehnungen Shakespeare's insbesondere aus Rabelais und einigen italienischen Dramatikern', *Jahrbuch der deutschen Shakespeare-Gesellschaft* 9 (1874): 195-232 (here as chapters 1 and 2); and 'Shakespeare und Giordano Bruno', *Jahrbuch der deutschen Shakespeare-Gesellschaft* 11 (1876): 97-139 (here as chapter 3).

Copyright
Wilhelm König, *Essays on Shakespeare and European Culture (1874 & 1876)*
Translation: Ritchie Robertson © 2024
Preface and editorial matter:
Elisabetta Tarantino © 2024
(We are grateful to the *Shakespeare Jahrbuch* for agreeing to us republishing this material)

Published by
abpb

ISBN (paperback) 978-1-8380002-3-3
ISBN (ebook) 978-1-8380002-7-1

Table of Contents

Preface   vii
(by Elisabetta Tarantino)

Chapter One   1
Shakespeare and Rabelais

Chapter Two   49
Shakespeare and Some Italian Dramatists

Chapter Three   71
Shakespeare and Giordano Bruno

List of Primary Works Cited   135
(when indication is not given within the text)

Index of Shakespeare Passages Cited   139

Preface

by Elisabetta Tarantino

This volume provides an English translation of two articles by Wilhelm König, a Shakespeare scholar who was active in Germany in the second half of the nineteenth century.[1] The two articles are 'Ueber die Entlehnungen Shakespeare's insbesondere aus Rabelais und einigen italienischen Dramatikern', *Jahrbuch der deutschen Shakespeare-Gesellschaft* 9 (1874): 195-232 (here as chapters 1 and 2); and 'Shakespeare und Giordano Bruno', *Jahrbuch der deutschen Shakespeare-Gesellschaft* 11 (1876): 97-139 (here as chapter 3).

We should also state what the present volume does *not* provide. Anyone for whom Wilhelm König himself is a subject of philological study will necessarily need to engage with the original articles, published in the *Shakespeare Jahrbuch* in 1874 (chapters 1 and 2 of this book) and 1876 (chapter

---

[1] All the library catalogues I have consulted list the wrong date of birth for this author, giving this as '1851', which would be instead that of Wilhelm König Jnr – see www.shakespearealbum.de/en/biographies/wilhelm-koenig.html (accessed 5 September 2023), or even the obviously irrelevant '1935', which refers to a twentieth-century novelist. As reported in the website just quoted, Wilhelm König Snr had already reached a certain age by the 1870s.

3).² Recourse to the original publications if using those articles as 'primary' rather than 'secondary' texts is a must, not least because, albeit in very few cases, we have omitted or silently corrected some obviously erroneous statements.

Having said that, as a by-product this volume may well provide a starting point or a window onto the way in which the issue of Shakespeare's knowledge and use of continental European sources was discussed in the second half of the nineteenth century. What we hope to present here is how, in many ways, this attitude was fairer and more open-minded than today's.

Our intention is, quite simply, to enable Shakespeare scholars who do not read German to become acquainted with what König had to say on the subject of the dramatist's engagement with certain European authors, especially (though by no means exclusively) with François Rabelais, Antonfrancesco Grazzini and Giordano Bruno. It is obvious to us that the issues discussed by König deserve to be brought once more to critics' attention. While his insights and information will need to be checked and updated against the latest research, it is still possible to find there some pointers that open up new avenues, or in some cases, as experienced by

---

² Such scholars would also, of course, need to examine König's book-length study, *Shakespeare als Dichter, Weltweiser und Christ. Durch Erläuterung von Vier seiner Dramen und eine Vergleichung mit Dante dargestellt* (Leipzig, 1873).

myself, provide independent support for finds that have been reached through different processes.[3]

König had no qualms about accepting that Shakespeare may have known and worked with both major and minor texts in French and Italian. If anything, in a few cases one might object that the common classical heritage plays too small a part in König's discussion, though even in this case often I would be inclined to see this more as possible instances of 'window reference' than a case of the classical antecedent simply cancelling out the European one adduced by König.[4] Thus, what at times comes across as disregard for probable common classical sources may be simply due to König's awareness that, despite his 'small Latin and less Greek', Shakespeare's relationship with the classics was undeniable, quite literally, from start to finish – i.e. from the appearance of a copy of Ovid's *Metamorphoses* on stage in *Titus Andronicus* to *The Tempest* and its, in Jonathan Bate's words, vigorously waved 'flag marked *Aeneid*' – and therefore went without saying.

---

[3] For an update on Shakespeare and sources, see John Drakakis, *Shakespeare's Resources* (Manchester, 2021); on imitation in general, see Colin Burrow, *Imitating Authors: Plato to Futurity* (Oxford, 2019). Ways in which König has provided useful hints for my own research are mentioned in chapter 2, note 12, and chapter 3, note 25.

[4] On 'window reference' see our note in Colin Burrow *et al.* (eds), *Imitative Series and Clusters from Classical to Early Modern Literature* (Berlin-Boston, 2020), pp. 303-305.

The chapter on Bruno is a particularly important example of the usefulness of bringing this material to non-Germanophones. König's seminal role in addressing the subject of Shakespeare and Bruno has long been known to more scholars than, it is legitimate to assume, have been easily able to engage with his texts first-hand. Furthermore, this chapter, even more than the others, illustrates how this material displays a more helpful attitude to certain themes than is the case in our own day.

The most remarkable thing about König's discussion of Shakespeare and philosophy at the start of his 1876 essay (chapter 3 in this volume) is the fact that it is taking place at all. This is because, as König himself points out, there is resistance to the idea of pragmatic Shakespeare as a 'philosophical' thinker. Nowadays, the dramatist's undoubted affiliation with Montaigne is as far as most critics would be prepared to travel in this direction (though not everyone would state as confidently as König that Shakespeare 'owned' a copy of the *Essays*). Even more remarkable, however, and a much-needed (and unfortunately forgotten) corrective to Frances Yates's magus and John Bossy's (later qualified) spy, is the fact that this discussion of Shakespeare and *philosophy* is seen as the necessary preamble to a discussion of Shakespeare and Giordano Bruno. As König writes: 'although [Shakespeare] certainly did not consider himself a philosopher, his profound understanding of human nature, especially of interacting and conflicting psychological forces, obliges us to regard him as a disciple and proponent of the branch of learning that is especially concerned with understanding the human mind and its relation to the world as a whole'. There we have it – the Shakespeare-Bruno relationship demystified, and in a way that goes straight to the heart of the question: what makes both Bruno and Shakespeare stand out from their contemporaries as quintessentially 'modern' figures is their 'profound understanding of interacting and conflicting psychological forces'.

* * *

A few words on our editorial choices. As already mentioned, we have silently intervened in the content, though only in a very few cases, and never in ways that distorted König's meaning. In rather more cases, we have added our own comments and clarifications, and these are clearly marked in square brackets. We have not made any attempts to update König's scholarship, except where the information was too immediately and obviously known to us to be ignored.

In supplying – and adding the original to – quotations we have attempted to adhere to a principle of usefulness rather than to a strict philological reproduction of König's text (though we have tended to keep his bibliographical references, simply adding our own as required). By far our most extensive intervention has been adding original-language texts (e.g. the original French for Rabelais quotations). The second biggest intervention has been to base all of Shakespeare quotations and references on the Norton collected works, including mentions of Act, scene and line numbers without the full quotation. Obviously, this applies also to the Index of Shakespeare passages that we have provided at the end of the volume. For both these kinds of intervention, i.e. the addition of inset quotations from the original and the revised Shakespeare text and references, we have foregone the use of square brackets in the interest of a clearer and uncluttered text. All our other interventions have been religiously indicated in square brackets (subject to human fallibility, for which we apologize in advance).

When we have provided English quotations from original sixteenth-century works we have modernized the spelling; for less-often-quoted texts in the original language we have tended to keep anything that König himself may have provided.

For Bruno quotations, as well as reproducing König's references to Adolf Wagner's nineteenth-century original-language edition, we have added references, and in some cases also the original text, from a more readily available and commonly used edition, i.e. the Gentile-Aquilecchia text listed in the

List of Primary Works Cited at the end of the volume.

In keeping with the pragmatic function of this volume there is no general bibliography that reproduces information already given in the notes. The Primary Works list only includes our own additions to the texts indicated by König himself, for which we have not given full bibliographical data within the text itself, once again with a view to keeping it as streamlined as possible. If no bibliographical reference is given for a primary text, the list at the end of the volume will tell the reader where the quotation is from, if the quotation has been added by us; if the reference is in neither, the text is as provided by König.

* * *

I should like to thank, first and foremost, Ritchie Robertson, who did an unobtrusively wonderful job of translating these two articles; the *Shakespeare Jahrbuch* for confirming that it was permissible for us to translate and publish these texts; Martin McLaughlin for providing general encouragement (and on-the-spot bouts of proof-reading); Hilary Gatti for pushing me onto the study of Shakespeare and Bruno, including making me aware of the importance of König in this field. As repeatedly acknowledged in the course of this study, quotations and line numbers follow the 1997 Norton Shakespeare edition.

Chapter One

Shakespeare and Rabelais

For a considerable time now, opinions concerning Shakespeare's merits and significance as a poet have been so far clarified that he is no longer considered an untutored genius, such as notable literary men of the last century described him. Yet even now – in a certain analogy to that obsolete judgement – a large number of his admirers, particularly including poets, see his greatness principally or solely in the poetic rendering of his chosen narrative materials, in the vigorous presentation of interesting and powerful characters, and especially in their happy disposition in accordance with the demands of the stage, even the stage of his time, although he has also received all manner of criticisms, some with reason and many without, from all these perspectives. These admirers refuse to acknowledge that the individual plays show any deeper intellectual content or artistic shaping. They see in him only the inspired poet, not the thinker, and attribute his creations more to poetic sensibility and inspiration than to craftsmanship and study. This is connected with the tendency – stronger, admittedly, in the past than at present – to minimize his acquaintance with languages and literature, and to assume that, in general, he neither learned nor used much from others. Of course it had to be acknowledged – and nobody familiar with the relevant source material will deny it – that Shakespeare normally did not invent the subject-matter of his plays, but adhered with some faithfulness to models from history, folk-tale or fiction, simply shaping them into a play. How much labour this cost him is of course easy to discern if one compares the novellas or histories he was following with the works into which he transformed them.

Such a comparison readily reveals the effect not only of the poetic sensitivity peculiar to him, but also of scrupulous study. Besides his essential sources, we also become acquainted with an increasing number of works that Shakespeare read and studied while composing, and from which he transposed individual scenes, individual images, indeed individual words, altered in varying degrees, into his own works.[1] On close examination, we cannot but admire the care and precision with which he treated the available materials, setting each in its proper place. No less must we marvel at the breadth of his knowledge of the native and foreign literature that he exploited for artistic purposes.

Even Shakespeare's contemporaries observed, probably more than his present-day critics, how he

---

[1] Several of these, particularly taken from Italian drama, are cited in Julius Leopold Klein, *Geschichte des Dramas*, 13 vols (Leipzig, 1865-76).

used literary productions even for the details of his own poetic creation, and this probably prompted the attack on him in Greene's well-known pamphlet for having 'beautified' himself 'with our feathers'.[2] This is obviously directed only at individual borrowings, for there is no doubt that the older adaptations of *Henry VI*, to which Greene's attack has been thought to refer, are likewise by Shakespeare, as Delius and Ulrici have demonstrated.[3] It is even less likely that the attack alludes to Shakespeare's imitation of his predecessors' manner in style and versification.[4] In fact, even Shakespeare's earlier works show a number of passages that are at least so similar to some in Marlowe's plays that Greene could find here a specious justification for his attack, which apparently referred only to the use of works by contemporaries.[5] His onslaught, however, was obviously motivated principally by vulgar envy of the more gifted and successful poet, and was soon withdrawn on incurring disapproval from others. If

---

[2] *A Groat's Worth of Wit Bought with a Million of Repentance*. Greene's passage is quoted in volume 4 of Nicolaus Delius's edition of *Shakespere's Werke* (Elberfeld, 1858), Introduction to *King Henry VI – Part 3*, pp. VIII-X.

[3] See, respectively, Delius's Introductions to the *Henry VI* plays, and specifically to *Part 3*, and Hermann Ulrici, *Shakespeares dramatische Kunst*, 3 vols in 1 (Leipzig, 1869), vol. 3, pp. 1-45.

[4] Cf. Delius, Introduction to *3 Henry VI*, p. X.

[5] Cf. Alexander Dyce, *The Works of Christopher Marlowe* (London, 1862), Introduction, p. 50n; Ulrici, *Shakespeares dramatische Kunst*, vol. 3, p. 36.

Greene had been able to demonstrate considerable and more unmistakable borrowings with a certain value, or if Shakespeare had already composed his *Winter's Tale*, which is known to be based on a story by Greene, his attack would undoubtedly have been much more forceful and specific. For this reason alone we may assume that at this early period Shakespeare, even in detail, relied less on other sources and more on his own imagination than in his later plays. After all, the plays for which no source has been demonstrated, e.g. *Titus Andronicus* and *Love's Labour's Lost*, belong mostly to his first period. In the later plays generally it is overwhelmingly clear, on the whole, that the relevant source is being followed. Admittedly, no such source has been identified, at least not with any certainty, for *The Tempest*, clearly one of his last plays, and it may be that we have here an entirely free imaginative creation, in which he wanted to present a concentrated symbolic image of humanity's culture and intellectual power. On the other hand, this very play contains such glaring detailed borrowings from other poets and writers that they would hardly be acceptable nowadays. Yet the ageing poet, whose reputation was now firmly established, could permit himself such liberties, and nothing is known of any serious offence that he aroused thereby.[6] For us, these examples confirm –

---

[6] Yet he has been attacked for plagiarizing the passage from Ben Jonson's *Volpone* cited in K. Elze, 'The Abfassungszeit

and therein lies their particular value – that Shakespeare incorporated even details from previous texts into his own works, so that we can follow his entire poetic method, revealed by the examination of his main sources, down into detail and have stronger grounds for concluding that he was imitating a prior source even in cases where the resemblance is slighter and may appear coincidental. For even when the resemblance is marked, such a conclusion can seldom be drawn with certainty, since many ideas, images and comparisons are naturally suggested by the subject-matter, and many dicta are the common property of the nation and occur in proverbial expressions and images. To identify a single utterance as a borrowing therefore requires us to proceed with great caution, and as a rule only recurring similarities will entitle us to assume, without further evidence, that Shakespeare made poetic use of the work in question, that he was influenced by it, or even that he knew it at all. On the other hand, Shakespeare used his materials and models with such freedom, combined what he found and what he invented in such close, indistinguishable organic unity, and he often subjects his material to such great changes that we must take care not to be deterred from discovering in

---

des Sturms', *Jahrbuch der Deutschen Shakespeare-Gesellschaft* 7 (1872): 29-47, on p. 33, and Thomas Tomkis's *Albumazar*, mentioned below.

the artistic form the elements originally imported from elsewhere.

First, in order to provide a basis for the present discussion, the passage from *The Tempest* must at least be mentioned, beginning with Gonzalo's description of a Utopian commonwealth, which is taken almost word for word, albeit with a few transpositions, from Montaigne's *Essays* (Book 1, chapter 30). We will then examine Prospero's beautiful speech in Act 5, scene 1 ('Ye elves of hills', ll. 33-57), an imitation of Ovid's *Metamorphoses* in Golding's translation, and finally Prospero's other, much-admired speech in Act 4, scene 1, which has an unmistakable model in the tragedy *Darius* by William Alexander, Earl of Stirling, first published in 1605 (all three passages are quoted by Delius in his Introduction to *The Tempest*).[7] We will quote only the last of these passages, in order to compare it with others. Shakespeare's lines run:

> Our revels now are ended. These our actors,
> As I foretold you, were all spirits, and
> Are melted into air, into thin air;
> And like the baseless fabric of this vision,
> The cloud-capped towers, the gorgeous palaces,
> The solemn temples, the great globe itself,
> Yea, all which it inherit, shall dissolve;
> And, like this insubstantial pageant faded,
> Leave not a rack behind. We are such stuff

---

[7] [Actually published in Edinburgh in 1603 and in London in 1604.]

> As dreams are made on, and our little life
> Is rounded with a sleep.
>> (*The Tempest* 4.1.148-158)[8]

Darius contains the words:

> Let greatness of her glassy scepters vaunt;
> Not scepters, no, but reeds, soon bruis'd, soon broken;
> And let this worldly pomp our wits enchant.
> All fades, and scarcely leaves behind a token.
> Those golden palaces, those gorgeous halls,
> With furniture superfluously fair,
> Those stately courts, those sky-encountring walls
> Evanish all like vapours in the air.
>> [William Alexander, *The Tragedy of Darius* 4.2; H1r-v]

Even a hasty comparison of the two passages makes it appear likely, not that Stirling reduced Shakespeare's energetic lines to the restriction of rhymed iambic pentameters, but rather that Shakespeare's lines are an expansion and enrichment of Stirling's words. It can be regarded as certain that *The Tempest* was composed later than Stirling's tragedy, and even Elze, who assigns *The Tempest* to an earlier date than any other interpreter, assumes that Shakespeare used this passage.[9] At all events it should be noted that we here have a borrowing from a poem by a contemporary that had

---

[8] [König quotes from Delius. However, for ease of retrieval by the reader, our Shakespeare quotations and line numbers are from the Norton Shakespeare.]

[9] Elze, 'Abfassungszeit', p. 29.

appeared only recently. In our view, however, Shakespeare also had to hand a passage from an earlier but still contemporary poet, Edmund Spenser, who died in 1598 – namely the following passage from *The Ruines of Time* (ll. 92-98):

> High towers, faire temples, goodly theatres,
> Strong walles, rich porches, princely palaces,
> Longe streets, brave houses, sacred sepulchers,
> Sure gates, sweet gardens, stately galleries,
> Wrought with faire pillours, and fine imageries,
> All those (oh pitty) now are turnd to dust,
> And over-growne with black oblivion's rust.

It could of course be that Stirling was imitating Spenser and that this accounts for the similarity between Spenser's lines and Shakespeare's, but the resemblance to the latter is greater than is the case with the passage from *Darius*. The towers, temples and theatres mentioned by Spenser at the outset do not appear in Stirling, but they do appear in Prospero's speech; although he does not speak explicitly of the theatre, his whole speech evokes the stage as an image of transience, and here Prospero may be seen not only as a character but as the actor and the poet. While Stirling's lines form two periods, the end of which is fairly distinctly repeated by Shakespeare at the beginning and in the middle, the passage quoted from Shakespeare differs widely from the other two passages towards the end. It contains an image, however, which is very similar to one in Sophocles' *Ajax* (ll. 125-126), though we would not like to maintain that it is borrowed thence:

> because I see that all of us who live are nothing but ghosts, or a fleeting shadow.

Shakespeare, too, often repeats this image, e.g. in *Hamlet* (3.1.62-63):

> To die, to sleep –
> No more

Measure for Measure (3.1.32-34):

> Thou hast nor youth nor age,
> But as it were an after-dinner's sleep
> Dreaming on both.[10]

And the closest resemblance to the passage from Sophocles is perhaps to be found in the line at *Macbeth* 5.5.23:

> Life's but a walking shadow, a poor player ...

Here again, as in the passage from *The Tempest*, the stage serves as an image of transience.

Among similar utterances by subsequent poets, we need only mention the concluding lines of

---

[10] A similar thought is expressed in Ossian; see the beginning of *The War of Inis-thona*: 'Our youth is like the dream of the hunter on the hill of heath. He sleeps in the mild beams of the sun; he awakes amidst a storm' [see under Macpherson in our List of Primary Works Cited; p. 203].

Act 2 [pp. 122-123] from Calderón's *Life is a Dream*:

> for, all of life is a dream,
> and even dreams are dreams.
>
> que toda la vida es sueño,
> y los sueños, sueños son.

From antiquity, see Pindar, 'A dream of a shadow | is man' [*Pythian* 8.95-96], which again recalls Hamlet's conversation about ambition.[11]

Even from what has just been quoted, it is easy to see how far we are led when we seek to pursue the same ideas in different poets, and how hard it is to establish definite borrowings or stimuli. We shall continue to examine passages in Shakespeare that suggest external influence, but we can deal only with a small selection and [in this and the next chapter] will give pride of place to passages from which we can deduce our poet's acquaintance with Rabelais and some lesser-known Italian dramatists.

Whenever Shakespeare's knowledge of the French satirist has been discussed, it has, to our knowledge, never been questioned. This assumption

---

[11] Cf. *Hamlet* 2.2.251-255:

> GUILDENSTERN ... for the very substance of the ambitious is merely the shadow of a dream.
> HAMLET A dream itself is but a shadow.
> ROSENCRANTZ Truly, and I hold ambition of so airy and light a quality that it is but a shadow's shadow.

is justified by the fact that the satirical novel *Gargantua and Pantagruel*, which is Rabelais's main literary legacy to posterity, was in Shakespeare's time a widely read book, even in England, and there appear by then to have been English translations of it. According to the Stationers' Register, as Steevens shows, books entitled *Gargantua his prophecie* and *The history of Gargantua* were printed in London in 1592 and 1594, and the book *Gargantua* is mentioned much earlier, in Robert Laneham's account of the Entertainment of Queen Elizabeth at Kenilworth Castle in 1575.[12] Rabelais is named as the author of these works in a satire by Joseph Hall.[13] Even Shakespeare himself, in *As You Like It* 3.2.205-206, mentions the titular name of Gargantua (a giant whom Rabelais uses to represent King Francis I),[14] and the name also occurs repeatedly in works by contemporaries (e.g. Ben Jonson's *Every Man in His Humour*, 2.2). However, that may not prove that Shakespeare knew Rabelais's novel, for the giant Gargantua is named and depicted in old, widely

---

[12] [Subsequently published as *Robert Laneham's Letter: Describing a Part of the Entertainment unto Queen Elizabeth at the Castle of Kenilworth in 1575*, various editions.]

[13] [Joseph Hall, *Virgidemiarum*, Book 2, Satire 1, 57-58.] Cf. *Meister Franz Rabelais ... Gargantua und Pantagruel aus dem Französischen verdeutscht, mit Einleitung und Anmerkungen ...*, edited by Gottlob Regis, 3 parts over 2 vols (Leipzig: Barth, 1832-1841), vol. 2, 'Anmerkungen', p. clxxi.

[14] CELIA You must borrow me Gargantua's mouth first,
 'tis a word too great for any mouth of this age's size.

disseminated French, English, and even German folk-tales and chap-books, and there is no doubt that Shakespeare was thoroughly familiar with this branch of literature.

On the other hand, a closer examination of Rabelais's novel confirms beyond doubt that Shakespeare knew it, used it here and there, and even studied it, however remote his works may be in poetic form, content and value from that of the Frenchman. Many passages in Shakespeare's works reveal similarities to passages in Rabelais, and, though they are mostly trivial, their frequent occurrence reinforces the conclusion that this is not accidental. In a few cases Shakespeare made comprehensive use of the French satirist's work as a model, albeit with such poetic freedom that the resemblance is not very striking and to our knowledge has not – at least in our time – been discussed. A precise comparison should therefore be justified and rewarding, even aside from the importance that literary history must attach to the proof of Rabelais's influence on Shakespeare. We quote here (from the final part of Book 3, chapter 3 of *Gargantua and Pantagruel*) the witty eulogy of borrowing with which Panurge, Pantagruel's companion, replies to the latter's criticism of him for running up debts:[15]

---

[15] [We quote here from the Urquhart and Motteux translation, which was published between 1653 and 1694 (we have modernized the use of italics and capitals). The French is

Well, to go yet further on, and possibly worse in your conceit, may Sanct Bablin, the good sanct, snatch me, if I have not all my lifetime held debt to be as an union or conjunction of the heavens with the earth, and the whole cement whereby the race of mankind is kept together; yea, of such vertue and efficacy, that, I say, the whole progeny of Adam would very suddenly perish without it. Therefore, perhaps, I do not think amiss, when I repute it to be the great soul of the universe, which (according to the opinion of the academicks) vivifyeth all manner of things. In confirmation whereof, that you may the better believe it to be so, represent unto your self, without any prejudicacy of spirit, in a clear and serene fancy, the idea and form of some other world than this; take if you please, and lay hold on the thirtieth of those which the philosopher Methrodorus did enumerate, wherein it is to be supposed there is no debtor or creditor, that is to say, a world without debts.

There amongst the planets will be no regular course, all will be in disorder. Jupiter reckoning himself to be nothing indebted unto Saturn, will go near to detrude him out of his sphere, and with the Homerick chain will be like to hang up the intelligences, gods, heavens, demons, heroes, devils, earth and sea together with the other elements. Saturn no doubt combining with Mars will reduce that so disturbed world into a chaos of confusion.

Mercury then would be no more subjected to the other planets; he would scorn to be any longer their Camillus, as he was of old termed in the Hetrurian tongue; for it is to be imagined that he is no way a debtor to them.

---

quoted from the Esmangart and Johanneau nine-volume edition (1823). See our List of Primary Works Cited for details of both editions.]

Venus will be no more venerable, because she shall have lent nothing. The moon will remain bloody and obscure: for to what end should the Sun impart unto her any of his light? He owed her nothing. Nor yet will the sun shine upon the earth, nor the stars send down any good influence, because the terrestrial globe hath desisted from sending up their wonted nourishment by vapours and exhalations, wherewith Heraclitus said the Stoicks proved Cicero maintained they were cherished and alimented. There would likeways be in such a world no manner of symbolization, alteration, nor transmutation amongst the elements; for the one will not esteem it self obliged to the other, as having borrowed nothing at all from it. Earth then will not become water, water will not be changed into air, of air will be made no fire, and fire will afford no heat unto the earth; the earth will produce nothing but monsters, titans, giants; no rain will descend upon it, nor light shine thereon; no wind will blow there, nor will there be in it any summer or harvest. Lucifer will break loose, and issuing forth of the depth of hell, accompanied with his Furies, fiends and horned devils, will go about to unnestle and drive out of heaven all the gods, as well of the greater as of the lesser nations. Such a world without lending, will be no better than a dog-kennel, a place of contention and wrangling, more unruly and irregular than that of the rector of Paris; a devil of an hurly-burly, and more disordered confusion, than that of the plagues of Douay. Men will not then salute one another; it will be but lost labour to expect aid or succour from any, or to cry, *Fire*, *Water*, *Murther*, for none will put to their helping hand. Why? He lent no money, there is nothing due to him. No body is concerned in his burning, in his shipwrack, in his ruine, or in his death; and that because he hitherto had lent nothing, and would never thereafter have lent any thing.

In short, faith, hope and charity would be quite banish'd from such a world; for men are born to relieve and assist one another; and in their stead should succeed and be introduced defiance, disdain and rancour, with the most execrable troop of all evils, all imprecations and all miseries. Whereupon you will think, and that not amiss, that Pandora had there spilt her unlucky bottle. Men unto men will be wolves; hobthrushers [= *werewolves; see below*] and goblins (as were Lycaon, Bellorophon, Nebuchodonosor), plunderers, highway robbers, cut-throats, rapperees, murtherers, payloners, assassinators, lewd, wicked, malevolent, pernicious haters, set against every body, like to Ismael, Metabus, or Timon the Athenian, who for that cause was named Misanthropos; in such sort, that it would prove much more easie in nature to have fish entertained in the air, and bullocks fed in the bottom of the ocean, than to support or tolerate a rascally rabble of people that will not lend. These fellows (I vow) do I hate with a perfect hatred; and if conform to the pattern of this grievous, peevish and perverse world which lendeth nothing, you figure and liken the little world, which is man, you will find in him a terrible justling coyle and clutter: the head will not lend the sight of his eyes to guide the feet and hands; the legs will refuse to bear up the body; the hands will leave off working any more for the rest of the members; the heart will be weary of its continual motion for the beating of the pulse, and will no longer lend his assistance; the lungs will withdraw the use of their bellows; the liver will desist from conveying any more blood through the veins for the good of the whole; the bladder will not be indebted to the kidneys, so that the urine thereby will be totally stopped. The brains, in the interim, considering this unnatural course, will fall into a raving dotage, and withhold all feeling from the sinews, and motion from the muscles: briefly, in such a world without order and array, owing nothing, lending nothing, and borrowing nothing, you would see a more dangerous conspiration than that which Esope exposed in his apologue. Such a world will perish undoubtedly; and not only perish, but perish very quickly. Were it Asculapius himself, his body would immediately rot, and the chafing soul, full of indignation, takes its flight to all the devils of hell after my money.

(Urquhart, vol. 2, pp. 26-29)

Bien pis y ha, je me donne a sainct Babolin, le bon sainct, en cas que toute ma vie je n'aye estimé debtes estre comme une connexion et colligence des cieulx et terre; ung entretenement unicque de l'humain lignaige (je dy sans lequel bien tost tous humains periroyent) estre par adventure celle grande ame de l'univers, laquelle, selon les academicques, toutes choses vivifie. Qu'ainsi soyt, representez vous en esprit serain l'idee et forme de quelque monde, prenez, si bon vous semble, le trentiesme de ceulx que imaginoyt le philosophe Metrodorus, ou le soixante et dix huyctieme de Petron: onquel ne soyt debteur ne crediteur aulcun. Ung monde sans debtes! la entre les astres ne sera cours regulier quiconcque: tous seront en desarroy. Jupiter, ne s'estimant debteur a Saturne, le depossedera de sa sphere, et avecques sa chaine homericque suspendra toutes les intelligences, dieux, cieulx, demons, genies, heroes, diables, terre, mer, tous elemens. Saturne se ralliera avec Mars, et mettront tout ce monde en perturbation. Mercure ne vouldra soy asservir es aultres; plus ne sera leur Camille, comme en langue hetrusque estoyt nommé; car il ne leur est en rien debteur. Venus ne sera veneree, car elle n'aura rien presté. La Lune restera sanglante et tenebreuse: a quel propous luy departiroyt le Soleil sa lumiere? il n'y estoyt en rien tenu. Le Soleil ne luyra sus leur terre; les astres ne y feront influence bonne, car la Terre desistoyt leur prester nourrissement par vapeurs et exhalations: desquelles disoyt Heraclitus, prouvoyent les stoiciens, Ciceron maintenoyt estre les estoilles alimentees. Entre les elemens ne sera symbolisation, alternation, ne transmutation aulcune. Car l'ung ne se reputera obligé a l'aultre: il ne luy avoyt rien presté. De terre ne sera faicte eaue; l'eaue en aer ne sera transmuee; de l'aer ne sera faict feu; le feu n'eschauffera la terre. La terre rien ne produyra que monstres, titanes, aloides, geans; il n'y pluyra pluye, n'y luyra lumiere, n'y ventera vent, n'y sera esté ne automne. Lucifer se desliera, et, sortant du profond d'enfer avec les furies, les poines et diables cornuz, vouldra deniger des cieulx tous les dieux, tant des majeurs comme des mineurs peuples. De cestuy monde rien ne prestant, ne sera que une chiennerie, que une brigue plus anomale que celle du recteur de Paris, que une diablerie plus confuse que celle des jeux de Doué. Entre les humains, l'ung ne saulvera l'aultre: il aura beau crier a l'ayde, au feu, a l'eaue, au meurtre, personne ne yra au secours. Pourquoy? Il n'avoyt rien presté, on ne lui debvoyt rien. Personne n'ha interest en sa conflagration, en son naufraige, en sa ruyne, en sa mort. Aussi bien ne prestoit il rien; aussi bien n'eust il pas apres rien presté. Brief, de cestuy monde seront bannies foy, esperance, charité: car les hommes sont nayz pour l'ayde et secours des hommes. En lieu d'elles succederont defiance, mespris, rancune, avecques la cohorte de tous maulx, toutes maledictions et toutes miseres. Vous penserez proprement que la eust Pandora versé sa bouteille. Les hommes seront loups es hommes; loups guaroux et lutins, comme furent Lycaon, Bellerophon, Nabugotdonosor; briguans, assassineurs, empoisonneurs, malfaisans, malpensans, malveillans, haine portans: ung chascun contre tous, comme Ismael, comme Metabus, comme Timon, athenien, qui, pour ceste cause, feut surnommé *misanthropos*. Si que chose plus facile en nature seroyt nourrir en l'aer les poissons, paistre les cerfz au fond de l'ocean, que supporter ceste truandaille de monde qui rien ne preste. Par ma foy, je les hay bien. Et si, au patron de ce fascheux et chagrin monde rien ne prestant, vous figurez l'aultre petit monde, qui est l'homme, vous y trouverez ung terrible tintamarre. La teste ne vouldra prester la veue de ses yeulx pour guider les piedz et les mains. Les pieds ne la daigneront porter; les mains cesseront travailler pour elle. Le cueur se faschera de tant se mouvoir pour les poulz des membres, et ne leur prestera plus. Le poulmon ne luy fera prest de ses soufflets. Le foye ne lui envoyera sang pour son entretien. La vessie ne vouldra estre debitrice aux roignons. L'urine sera supprimee. Le cerveau, considerant ce train desnaturé, se mettra en resuerie, et ne baillera sentement es nerfz, ne mouvement es muscles. Somme, en ce monde desrayé, rien ne debvant, rien ne prestant, rien ne empruntant, vous voyrez une conspiration plus pernicieuse que n'a figuré Esope en son apologue. Et perira sans doubte, non perira seullement, mais bien tost perira, feust ce Esculapius mesme. Et ira soubdain le corps en putrefaction: l'ame toute indignee prendra course a tous les diables, apres mon argent.

(Esmangart, vol. 4, pp. 252-257)

From this passage, in our view, Shakespeare made characteristic use of particular parts at three points in various dramas. The first is Ulysses' exhortation to the other Greek commanders in *Troilus and Cressida* (1.3.94-124):

> But when the planets
> In evil mixture to disorder wander,
> What plagues and what portents, what mutiny?
> What raging of the sea, shaking of earth?
> Commotion in the winds, frights, changes, horrors
> Divert and crack, rend and deracinate
> The unity and married calm of states
> Quite from their fixture. O when degree is shaked,
> Which is the ladder to all high designs,
> The enterprise is sick. How could communities,
> Degrees in schools, and brotherhoods in cities,
> Peaceful commerce from dividable shores,

> The primogenity and due of birth,
> Prerogative of age, crowns, sceptres, laurels
> But by degree stand in authentic place?
> Take but degree away, untune that string,
> And hark what discord follows. Each thing meets
> In mere oppugnancy. The bounded waters
> Should lift their bosoms higher than the shores
> And make a sop of all this solid globe;
> Strength should be lord of imbecility,
> And the rude son should strike his father dead.
> Force should be right – or rather, right and wrong,
> Between whose endless jar justice resides,
> Should lose their names, and so should justice too.
> Then everything includes itself in power,
> Power into will, will into appetite;
> And appetite, an universal wolf,
> So doubly seconded with will and power,
> Must make perforce an universal prey,
> And last eat up himself.

The resemblances between Ulysses' speech and Rabelais lie, admittedly, less in details than in the general conception of the mutual dependence of the heavenly bodies, of the emergence of disorder, and in the whole manner of rhetorical delivery. The only relevant detail is the 'werewolves' ('loups guaroux') that occur in Rabelais and may have prompted the last lines of the above quotation, unless it was the she-wolf at the opening of Dante's *Inferno*, or unless this widespread image, to which Shakespeare has given an unusually bold turn, was stimulated by some other source. For Shakespeare's above-quoted lines, however, Rabelais's novel provides another, somewhat clearer model. In Book 4, chapter 26 [vol.

3, p. 12 in Le Motteux's translation], mention is made of a dark forest ['obscure forest', Esmangart, vol. 6, p. 245] where the heroes dwell, and then the text runs:

> At the death of every one of them we commonly hear in the forest loud and mournful groans, and the whole land is infested with pestilence, earthquakes, inundations and other calamities; the air with fogs and obscurity, and the sea with storms and hurricanes. What you tell us seems to me likely enough, said Pantagruel; for as a torch or candle, as long as it hath life enough and is lighted, shines round about, disperses its light, delights those that are near it, yields them its service and clearness, and never causes any pain or displeasure; but as soon as 'tis extinguished, its smoak and evaporation infects the air, offends the by-standers, and is noisome to all; so, as long as those noble and renowned souls inhabit their bodies, peace, profit, pleasure, and honour never leave the places where they abide; but as soon as they leave them, both the continent and the adjacent islands are annoyed with great commotions; in the air, fogs, darkness, thunder, hail, tremblings, pulsations, arietations of the earth, storms and hurricanes at sea, together with sad complaints amongst the people, broaching of religions, changes in governments, and ruins of commonwealths.
>
> Au trespas d'ung chascun d'iceulx ordinairement oyons nous par la forest grandes et pitoyables lamentations, et voyons en terre pestes, vimeres et afflictions, en l'aer troublement et tenebres: en mer tempeste et fortunal.
> Il y ha, dist Pantagruel, de l'apparence en ce que dictes. Car comme la torche ou la chandelle tout le temps qu'elle est vivente et ardente, luist ez assistants, esclaire tout au tour, delecte ung chascun, et a chascun expose son service et sa clarté, ne faict mal ne

> desplaisir a personne: sus l'instant qu'elle est estaincte, par sa fumee et evaporation elle infectionne l'aer, elle nuit es assistants et a ung chascun desplaist. Ainsy est il de ces ames nobles et insignes. Tout le temps qu'elles habitent leur corps, est leur demeure pacifique, utile, delectable, honorable: sus l'heure de leur discession, communement adviennent par les isles, et continents grans troublements en l'aer, tenebres, fouldres, gresles: en terre concussions, tremblements, estonnements: en mer fortunal et tempestes, avecques lamentations des peuples, mutations des religions, transports des royaulmes, et eversions des republicques.
>
> (Esmangart, vol. 6, p. 246)

Both passages quoted here from Rabelais, especially the latter, also resemble Gloucester's words in *King Lear* (1.2.99-106):[16]

> ... Love cools, friendship falls off, brothers divide; in cities, mutinies; in countries, discord; in palaces, treason; and the bond cracked 'twixt son and father ... Machinations, hollowness, treachery, and all ruinous disorders, follow us disquietly to our graves.

There is no need to enlarge on how far Shakespeare is throughout superior to Rabelais in power and beauty, and here too we must recall the even greater, truly titanic power with which the theme treated in these extracts, the upheavals in which nature dissolves into chaos, is given poetic expression in the famous storm scene in *King Lear* (beginning of Act 3). To be fair to the French satirist, we must of course acknowledge that he presents this theme in the context of a calm, even jocular conversation,

---

[16] [We quote from the 'conflated text'].

where poetic elevation would have been inappropriate, and Shakespeare's treatment of the same subject differs widely according to the occasion and the emotions of the speaker.

With regard to the originality of the idea, our poet seems to have borrowed from Rabelais especially in the second passage now to be mentioned, and indeed Rabelais's original defence of borrowing invited such an approach. The idea of heavenly bodies borrowing from each other is repeated in *Timon of Athens* with a variation whereby the world and the heavenly bodies are represented as stealing from one another. Timon says (4.3.428-437):

> I'll example you with thievery.
> The sun's a thief, and with his great attraction
> Robs the vast sea. The moon's an arrant thief,
> And her pale fire she snatches from the sun.
> The sea's a thief, whose liquid surge resolves
> The moon into salt tears. The earth's a thief,
> That feeds and breeds by a composture stol'n
> From gen'ral excrement. Each thing's a thief.
> The laws, your curb and whip, in their rough power
> Has unchecked theft.

Moreover, poem 21 in the *Anacreontea* [in the Renaissance thought to be by Anacreon himself] displays similar boldness in the treatment of the relations among the heavenly bodies, though it was probably the learned Rabelais rather than Shakespeare who had the Greek poet to hand in such passages:

> The black earth drinks, the trees drink it. The sea drinks the torrents, the sun the sea, the moon the sun. Why fight with me, my friends, if I too want to drink?

The third passage in which Shakespeare was influenced by the above chapter from Rabelais is, in our view, the speech made by Menenius Agrippa to the rebellious citizens at the very beginning of *Coriolanus* (1.1). Plutarch, Shakespeare's actual source for the Roman plays, gives only a very brief account, as does Livy (Book 2, chapter 32).[17] Shakespeare's version, however, is far fuller. It was probably in the following lines, above all, that he had Rabelais's account in mind:

> Your most grave belly was deliberate,
> Not rash like his accusers, and thus answered:
> 'True, is it, my incorporate friends', quoth he,
> 'That I receive the general food at first
> Which you do live upon, and fit it is,
> Because I am the storehouse and the shop
> Of the whole body. But, if you do remember,
> I send it through the rivers of your blood
> Even to the court, the heart, to th' seat o'th' brain;
> And through the cranks and offices of man
> The strongest nerves and small inferior veins
> From me receive that natural competency
> Whereby they live ...'
> (*Coriolanus* 1.1.117-129)

The same material, moreover, is repeated more fully in the next chapter of *Gargantua and Pantagruel*,

---

[17] See Delius's introduction to *Coriolanus*, in part 2 of his edition.

which describes the other side of the coin, the happiness of lending to each other, but no more similarities to Shakespeare's words are apparent than in the extract above. Shakespeare at any rate reduced the development of the image to a suitable length, taking into account that Menenius had to speak to the Roman proletariat quite unambiguously.

Further confirmation that Shakespeare, in the passages just mentioned, had this chapter from Rabelais to hand comes from the manner in which his contemporaries teased him for such a borrowing. The relevant passage, which for this reason is highly interesting, occurs in the comedy *Albumazar* (1615), by Thomas Tomkis, at the very beginning of the first act; it will now be reproduced so that the reader may compare it carefully to the passage above, since it contains an obviously deliberate conflation of the elements of Shakespeare's lines in *Timon* and *Coriolanus* with the corresponding speech in Rabelais:

> ALBUMAZAR ...
> Most trades and callings much participate
> Of yours; though smoothly gilt with th'honest title
> Of merchant, lawyer, or such like: the learned
> Only excepted; and he's therefore poor.
> HARPAX And yet he steals one author from another.
> This poet is that poet's plagiary,
> And he a third's, till they end all in Homer.
> ALBUMAZAR And Homer filched it all from an Egyptian priestess.

> The world's a theatre of theft. Great rivers
> Rob smaller brooks; and them the ocean.
> And in this world of ours, this microcosm,
> Guts from the stomach steal, and what they spare,
> The meseraics filch, and lay it in the liver:
> Where (lest it should be found), turned to red nectar,
> 'Tis by a thousand thievish veins conveyed
> And hid in flesh, nerves, bones, muscles and sinews,
> In tendons, skin and hair, so that, the property
> Thus altered, the theft can never be discovered.
> Now all these pilferies, couched and composed in order,
> Frame thee and me. Man's a quick mass of thievery.
> RONCA Most philosophical Albumazar!
> HARPAX *I thought these parts had lent and borrowed mutual.*
> ALBUMAZAR Say they do so: 'tis done with full intention
> Ne'er to restore, and that's flat robbery.
>   (*Albumazar* 1.1)

The line that we have italicized conveys clearly that Tomkis, by referring to Rabelais's 'lending', applying Timon's theory of 'stealing', and adopting Shakespeare's scattered images, is signaling that he has discovered our poet's borrowings from Rabelais and is subtly ridiculing them. To be sure, the beginning of the conversation quoted is fairly crude, but it is phrased in such general terms that it cannot be applied directly to Shakespeare. The mockery that follows, however, is wittily formulated, for Tomkis himself employs the same borrowing and simultaneously draws attention so naturally and with such seeming innocence to the slight difference between Rabelais's version and Timon's. If any further proof is required that Shakespeare is being alluded to here, it emerges from the relation between the content of the first few lines of the *Albumazar* passage and the following words of Timon, which occur not far from those quoted above and have no counterpart in Rabelais:

> Yet thanks I must you con
> That you are thieves professed, that you work not
> In holier shapes; for there is boundless theft
> In limited professions.
>   (*Timon of Athens* 4.3.418-421)

Finally, in the sentence 'The world's a theatre of theft' Tomkis seems to be alluding specifically to Shakespeare and his 'All the world's a stage' in *As You Like It* (2.7.138). At the same time, there can be no doubt that he also had Rabelais in his sights. For example, Tomkis has taken from Panurge's speech the microcosm, which goes unmentioned by Shakespeare.

    Of the author of *Albumazar* we know only that he was at Trinity College, Cambridge, where in 1614 his play was performed before the King. No other poetic works by Tomkis are known;[18] since this play shows some dramatic skill, he may have died young, or this may have been the only occasion, prompted perhaps by the royal visit, that

---

[18] [The allegorical comedy *Lingua* (1607) is now also attributed to Tomkis.]

he tried his hand at dramatic poetry. Nor is it an original composition; it was probably not offered as such, for it is a fairly faithful version of Giovanni Battista Della Porta's comedy *L'astrologo*, which appeared in Venice in 1606, and presents the same characters under the same names as the Italian play.[19]

The fable related by Menenius Agrippa can be traced back to Aesop, as Rabelais too indicates. Rabelais also quotes this in another passage that, in our view, Shakespeare again used for his own purposes. In Book 3, chapter 15 (vol. 2, p. 78), Rabelais writes:

---

[19] [The equally amusingly ironic opening conversation in *L'astrologo* among these characters does not contain a 'philosophical' excursus such as that quoted here from *Albumazar*.] In an entirely different manner from Tomkis, the images from the *Timon* and *Coriolanus* passages quoted above reappear together in Milton's *Paradise Lost* (5.414-426):

> For know, whatever was created, needs
> To be sustained and fed; of elements
> The grosser feeds the purer, earth the sea,
> Earth and the sea feed air, the air those fires
> Ethereal, and as lowest first the moon;
> Whence in her visage round those spots, unpurg'd
> Vapours not yet into her substance turned.
> Nor doth the Moon no nourishment exhale
> From her moist continent to higher orbs.
> The sun that light imparts to all, receives
> From all his alimental recompence
> In humid exhalations, and at even
> Sups with the ocean.

It is a very ordinary and common thing amongst men to conceive, foresee, know and presage the misfortune, bad luck or disaster of another; but to have the understanding, providence, knowledge and prediction of a man's own mishap is very scarce and rare to be found any where. This is exceeding judiciously and prudently deciphered by Aesop in his apologues, who there affirmeth, that every man in the world carrieth about his neck a wallet, in the fore-bag whereof were contained the faults and mischances of others, always exposed to his view and knowledge; and in the other scrip thereof, which hangs behind, are kept the bearer's proper transgressions, and inauspicious adventures, at no time seen by him, nor thought upon, unless he be a person that hath a favourable aspect from the heavens.

Chose bien commune et vulgaire entre les humains est le malheur d'aultruy entendre, preveoir, congnoistre et predire. Mais o que chose rare est son mal heur propre predire, cognoistre, preveoir et entendre! Et que prudentement le figura Æsope en ses apologues, disant, chascun homme en ce monde naissant une bezace au col porter, au sachet de laquelle devant pendent sont les faultes et malheurs d'aultruy, toujours exposees a nostre veue et cognoissance: au sachet derriere pendent sont les faultes et malheurs propres: et jamais ne sont veues ne entendues, fors de ceulx qui des cieulx ont le benevole aspect.
   (Esmangart, vol. 4, p. 376)

The only ancient writer who mentions Aesop's parable, and then only briefly, is Stobaeus.[20]

---

[20] Αἴσωπος ἔφη δύο πήρας ἕκαστον ἡμῶν φέρειν, τὴν μὲν ἔμπροσθεν, τὴν δὲ ὄπισθεν καὶ εἰς μὲν τὴν ἔμπροσθεν, ἀποτιθέναι τὰ τῶν ἄλλων ἁμαρτήματα εἰς δε τὴν ὄπισθεν, τὰ

Shakespeare, who is hardly likely to have known this writer, must have taken the curious image from Rabelais, applying it in *Troilus and Cressida* (3.3.139-144) as follows:

> Time hath, my lord,
> A wallet at his back, wherein he puts
> Alms for oblivion, a great-sized monster
> Of ingratitudes. Those scraps are good deeds past,
> Which are devoured as fast as they are made,
> Forgot as soon as done.

The passage just quoted provides, in our view, a perfect demonstration that Shakespeare knew and used Rabelais's novel. Admittedly, we cannot point to any situations, scenes, or characters showing that Shakespeare was influenced by the witty Frenchman. Falstaff does in some features recall Rabelais's Panurge, but he is essentially different from the latter and these features are not exactly characteristic.[21] On the other hand, we can cite many original formulations and images from Rabelais that recur in Shakespeare, and even if we do not assume in every case that Shakespeare's words can be traced back to Rabelais, we do not wish to ignore such similarities, both in order to let others consider them

---

εαυτῶν, διο και ούδε καθορώμεν αυτά. [*Joannis Stobæi Florilegium* 23.6, vol. 1, p. 425].

[21] French writers have long recognized a kinship in comic spirit between Shakespeare and Rabelais. For instance, Sainte-Beuve said of Rabelais: 'Il est notre Shakspeare dans le comique' (*Tableau historique et critique de la poésie française et du théatre français au seizième siècle* [Paris, 1843, p. 274]).

and also to attach to them other mentions that belong in this context. We are induced to fulfil the latter purpose by the following note:

1. In Rabelais's novel (Book 4, chapter 54; vol. 3, p. 81) the text reads: 'we are a plain downright sort of people, as God would have it, and call figs, figs; plumbs, plumbs; and pears, pears.' Similarly Polonius says in *Hamlet* (2.2.87-90):

   My liege, and madam, to expostulate
   ...
   Why day is day, night night, and time is time,
   Were nothing but to waste night, day, and time.

   Here, however, in our view, Shakespeare was thinking of a passage in the writings of Giordano Bruno.[22] In the dedication to Philip Sidney that he prefaced to the *Spaccio della bestia trionfante*, a work printed and published in London during Bruno's residence there (1583-1585), the author says of himself: 'Here Giordano speaks in the common manner, calls things by their right names, uses the proper expression for things to which nature gave their proper character;

---

[22] Cf. Benno Tschischwitz, *Shakspere-Forschungen*, 3 parts (Halle, 1868), Part 1, *Shakspere's Hamlet*, pp. 68-69.

[...] he calls bread bread, wine wine, the head head, the foot foot', etc.[23]

The resemblance to the *Hamlet* passage consists only in the repetition of the same word, since Bruno's disquisition, which is continued in the same manner at undue length, contains none of the objects mentioned by Polonius. We find ourselves, however, compelled to assume Shakespeare's indebtedness by the fact that Giordano Bruno's philosophical disquisitions as a whole, and in various details, recall Hamlet's utterances and outlook, as well as individual words spoken by Polonius. In addition, the manner in which Shakespeare shortened the Nolan's mode of expression and added the words

> Therefore, since brevity is the soul of wit
> (*Hamlet* 2.2.91)

suggests that it was the Nolan's excessive verbosity that inspired these words at this point, so that both he and Polonius are being humorously mocked.

However, it must not go unmentioned that both Rabelais and Bruno, and hence

---

[23] [Qua Giordano parla per volgare, nomina liberamente, dona il proprio nome a chi la natura dona il proprio essere ... chiama il pane, pane; il vino, vino; il capo, capo; il piede, piede ... (Bruno, *Dialoghi italiani*, ed. Gentile-Aquilecchia, vol. 2, p. 551).]

Shakespeare too, had models for these words in other writers and proverbs.[24]

2. When the King asks where Polonius is, Hamlet replies (4.3.33-34):

> In heaven. Send thither to see. If your messenger find him not there, seek him i' th' other place yourself.

The last phrase occurs several times in Rabelais's novel, namely:

> *Hagios ho theos.* If thou be of God speak: if thou be of the other spirit avoid hence, and get thee going
> (Book 1, chapter 35; vol. 1, pp. 102-103)

> *Hagios ho theos.* Si tu es de dieu, sy parle: si tu es de l'aultre, sy t'en va.
> (Esmangart, vol. 2, pp. 153-154)

> help me in the name of God, seeing you will not in the name of the other spirit
> (Book 1, chapter 42; vol. 1, p. 122)

> Aidez moy de par dieu, puisque de par l'aultre ne voulez.
> (Esmangart, vol. 2, p. 236)

---

[24] In his notes to Rabelais, vol. 2, p. 715, Regis refers to Erasmus quoting Aristophanes in the *Adagia* (rusticanus sum, et ligonem ligonem appello). He further mentions Robert Burton, *The Anatomy of Melancholy*, a text that Shakespeare is believed to have known, where we find the proverbial phrase 'I call a spade a spade'. Boileau's play on the saying is well known: J'appelle un chat un chat, et Rollet un fripon.

> Come, pluck up a good heart, speak the truth, and shame the devil. Be cheery, my lads, and if you are for me, take me off three or five bumpers to the best, while I make an halt of the first part of the sermon; then answer my question. If you are not, avaunt! avoid Satan!
> (Book 5, Prologue; vol. 3, pp. 121-122)

> N'ayez honte, faictes confusion à Her der Tyfel, ennemy de paradis, ennemy de verité; couraige, enfants, si estes des miens, beuvez trois ou cinq fois pour la premiere partie du sermon, puis respondez a ma demande; si estes de l'aultre, Avalisque Satanas.
> (Esmangart, vol. 7, pp. 220-221)

Such expressions are alien to the Bible, and from earlier times we know only a few places where anything even remotely similar occurs.[25] Later, however, the expression is frequent. This can be explained by people's reluctance to name the Evil One and to talk of the Devil.[26]

---

[25] Already in pre-Christian times we find in Pindar (*Pythian* 3.34-35): δαίμων δ' ἕτερος | ἐς κακὸν τρέψαις ἐδαμάσσατό νιν [which König interprets, differently from some modern editors, as applying to Apollo's anger towards Coronis, i.e. as: 'He was pushed | by the other spirit, which turned him to evil']. In Pulci's *Morgante maggiore* (written in 1481-1488) we read: Quivi già i campi l'uno a l'altro accosto, | Da ogni parte si gridava forte: | Chi vuol lesso Macon, chi l'altro arrosto (26.49).

[26] The last quoted passage from Rabelais closely resembles the expression used in another French satirical novel: Si tu es de Dieu, parle, si tu es de l'autre, va-t'en! (Théodore Agrippa d'Aubigné, *Les Aventures du baron de Faeneste*, Part 3, chapter 24 [p. 214]). According to the first edition, d'Aubigné's *Faeneste* dates from 1617, which is confirmed by

some facts alluded to in the text, but at that time the author was aged 65 and it is possible that parts of it had become known earlier, at the time when Shakespeare was writing. [In fact, the passage in question is from the very end of the third part, which was published in 1619, two years after the first two. It stands to reason that if this part had been ready earlier it would have been published together with the first two. The 'accommodate' discussion below does have some merit, though. And in relation to d'Aubigné's particular version of the turn of phrase under discussion, see also *Hamlet* 1.4.21-25: 'Be thou a spirit of health or goblin damned ... Be thy intents wicked or charitable ... I will speak to thee'. Could the influence have gone the other way round? Might the Huguenot d'Aubigné have known of the work of an English playwright that critics are increasingly beginning to read in the light of the religious crisis of the time?] We mention this work particularly because it contains another curious expression that in Shakespeare gives rise to a jocular but lengthy debate and for which no other source can be found. In Book 1, chapter 1 of this novel Faeneste recounts: *J'ai quitté à Surgères mes roussens, en la compenio de Monsur de Catelouz, qui m'en aboit accommodé. Ils sont miens et ne sont pas miens; on nous les garde pour une autre vegade.* ('I left my horses at Surgères with M. de Catelouz, who had accommodated me with them. They are and are not mine; they are being kept for me to use some other time.') Regarding the word that interests us here, *accommodé*, an editor (Jacob Le Duchat, 1729) remarks: 'Ce mot étoit nouveau en ce sens & c'est pour cette raison que l'Auteur le préte à un éventé de Courtisan' (i.e. the Lord Faeneste, from the Greek for 'to seem', a Gascon who affects a lofty style). This word is used in the same sense by Bardolph and Justice Shallow (likewise braggarts of sorts), and practically worked to death, in the following exchange, which comes after Shallow's inquiry after Falstaff and his 'lady' (*2 Henry IV* 3.2.61-73):

> BARDOLPH Sir, pardon, a soldier is better accommodated than with a wife.
> SHALLOW It is well said, in faith, sir, and it is well said indeed, too. 'Better accommodated' – it is good; yea, indeed is it. Good phrases are surely, and ever were,

3. In Rabelais's novel, when drowning is spoken of, we read:

> thou hast been afraid during the storm, without cause or reason; for thou wert not born to be drowned, but rather to be hang'd, and exalted in the air, or to be roasted in the midst of a jolly

---

> very commendable. 'Accommodated' – it comes of '*accommodo*'. Very good, a good phrase.
> BARDOLPH Pardon, sir, I have heard the word – 'phrase' call you it? – By this day, I know not the phrase; but I will maintain the word with my sword to be a soldier-like word, and a word of exceeding good command, by heaven. 'Accommodated'; that is, when a man is, as they say, accommodated; or when a man is being whereby a may be thought to be accommodated; which is an excellent thing.

Later, Shakespeare used the word again, but in a serious speech. King Lear says, on seeing the disguised Edgar, who is actually naked: 'Thou art the thing itself; unaccommodated man is no more but such a poor, bare, forked animal as thou art' (*King Lear* 3.4.98-100). Moreover, *Measure for Measure*, in the Duke's speech on the value of life, has: 'For all th'accommodations that thou bear'st | Are nursed by baseness' (3.1.14-15), where 'accommodations' clearly means all the additions that make life agreeable. The word was only gradually establishing itself; it is used also by Ben Jonson to convey affectation, as appears from this passage from *Every Man In His Humour* (1.5.102-105): 'Hostess, accommodate us with another bedstaff here quickly. Lend us another bedstaff! The woman does not understand the words of action.'

In Esmangart's 1823 edition of Rabelais, quoted above, we find the following editorial remark in connection with the passage in question: 'Les Bretons, encore aujourd'hui, n'osent pas nommer le diable, ni une bête malfaisante, par son nom, de crainte que le diable ou la bête ne vienne les emporter' (vol. 2, p. 155).

bonfire ... Friend Panurge, said Fryar Jhon [sic], I pray thee never be afraid of water, thy life for mine, thou art threatn'd with a contrary element.
(Book 4, chapter 24; vol. 3, pp. 8-9)

durant la tempeste tu as eu paour sans cause et sans raison. Car tes destinees fatales ne sont a perir en eaue. Tu seras hault en l'aer certainement pendu, ou bruslé guaillard comme ung pere ... Panurge mon amy, dist frere Jean, n'aye jamais paour de l'eaue, je t'en prie. Par element contraire sera ta vie terminee.
(Esmangart, vol. 6, pp. 225, 227)

In *The Tempest* Shakespeare exploits this joke at considerable, indeed excessive length, but it is justified as a means of characterizing the long-winded Gonzalo. The latter says:[27]

I have great comfort from this fellow. Methinks he hath no drowning mark upon him; his complexion is perfect gallows. Stand fast, good Fate, to his hanging. Make the rope of his destiny our cable, for our own doth little advantage. If he be not born to be hanged, our case is miserable.
(*The Tempest* 1.1.25-29)

I'll warrant him for drowning, though the ship were no stronger than a nutshell and as leaky as an unstanched wench.
(1.1.41-43)

---

[27] This whole scene may have had among its models the description of a storm at sea and the terror of the ship's crew in Book 4, chapters 14-21 of *Gargantua and Pantagruel*.

> He'll be hanged yet,
> Though every drop of water swear against it
> And gape at wid'st to glut him.
> (1.1.52-54)

> I prophesied if a gallows were on land
> This fellow could not drown.
> (5.1.220-221)

The same pronouncement occurs in the early *Two Gentlemen of Verona* (1.1.136-138):

> Go, go, be gone, to save your ship from wreck,
> Which cannot perish having thee aboard,
> Being destined to a drier death on shore.

Hence, if Shakespeare did borrow this joke from Rabelais's novel, he must have known it at a fairly early date. He may also have known the joke as a witticism current among the people, as it still is. At that time however, such a joke was probably still new or little known, otherwise the poet would hardly have repeated it so often.

4. A few of the jokes practised and spoken by Falstaff and his companions can also be found in Rabelais. In Book 4, chapter 63 of his novel, Eusthenes plays with his fingers on a long culverin, as though on a trump-marine. Falstaff likewise enters the Boar's Head Tavern 'playing upon his truncheon like a fife' (*1 Henry IV* 3.3.79 s.d.).

In Book 4, chapter 49 Homenaz, one of Pantagruel's companions, says:

> 'Tis enjoyn'd us by our Holy Decretals to visit churches first, and taverns after. Therefore, not to decline that fine institution, let us go to church; we shall afterwards go to feast our selves. Man of God, quoth Fryar Jhon, do you go before, we'll follow you; you spoke in the matter properly and like a good Christian; 'tis long since we saw any such.
> (Vol. 3, p. 65)

> par nos sainctes decretales nous est enjoinct et commandé visiter premier les ecclises que les cabarets. Pourtant ne declinants de ceste belle institution allons a l'ecclise, apres irons bancqueter. Homme de bien, dist frere Jean, allez devant, nous vous suivrons; vous en avez parlé en bons termes et en bon christian: ja long temps ha que n'en avions veue ...
> (Esmangart, vol. 7, p. 17)

Similarly, Falstaff says of himself (*1 Henry IV* 3.3.4-9):

> Well, I'll repent, and that suddenly, while I am in some liking. I shall be out of heart shortly, and then I shall have no strength to repent. An I have not forgotten what the inside of a church is made of, I am a peppercorn, a brewer's horse – the inside of a church! Company, villainous company, hath been the spoil of me.

Just as Falstaff calls himself and his comrades 'squires of the night's body', 'Diana's foresters', 'minions of the moon' (*1*

Henry IV 1.2.21-26), so Rabelais introduces characters of every profession and occupation, including foresters, huntsmen, fools, swindlers, as subject to the moon:

> Huntsmen, Faulkners, Posts, Salters, Lunatics,
> Fools, Shallow-brains, Obstinates,
> Fantastical people, Carriers, Horse-coursers,
> Lacquies, Brokers, Tennis-players,
> Glaziers, Light horsemen, Ferry-men,
> Seamen, Grooms ...
>   (Pantagruel's Prognostication, chapter 5)

> bisouars, veneurs, chasseurs, asturciers, faulconniers, courriers, saulniers, lunaticques, fols, escervelez, acariastres, esventez, courratiers, postes, laquets, nacquets, voyriers, estradiots, riverains, matelots, chevaulcheurs d'escurie, alleboteurs ...
>   (Esmangart, vol. 8, p. 299)

The 'horn of abundance', of which Falstaff speaks in *2 Henry IV* 1.2.40, through which woman's wantonness can be seen, may well owe its origin to the transparent horn that Rabelais mentions in Book 3 at the end of chapter 13, likewise applying it to a deceived husband, for the image is somewhat peculiar, despite Shakespeare's many jests about husbands being made to wear horns.

    Finally, Rabelais's description of a glutton (Book 5, chapter 17) sweating grease and bursting his belly recalls Falstaff with his 'girdle', 'guts' and 'flesh' (*1 Henry IV*

3.3.140-153), or 'pissing [his] tallow' (*The Merry Wives of Windsor* 5.5.12).

5. The French satirist's novel is packed with coarse expressions and obscene jokes. One of the wittiest is the story of the jealous husband who dreams that the Devil gives him a ring that will guarantee his wife's virtue as long as he keeps it on his finger (Book 3, chapter 28). The story must have been very popular, for it is still told without any thought of Rabelais, who himself took it from older works.[28] It is alluded to, in our

---

[28] The earliest writer to tell this story is said to be the Florentine Poggio (d. 1459), whose *Facetiae* include it as no. 183 under the title *Visio Francisci Philelphi*. It is then recounted in the eleventh of the *Cent nouvelles nouvelles* which were assembled in the reign of Louis XI of France (after 1461). Finally, before Shakespeare, it was adapted by Ariosto in his fifth Satire, and his conclusion broadly resembles the closing words quoted below from Rabelais:

> Par che 'l diavolo allor gli ponga in dito
> uno annello, e ponendolo gli dica:
> 'Fin che ce 'l tenghi, esser non puoi tradito.'
> Lieto ch'omai la sua senza fatica
> potrà guardar, si sveglia il mastro, e truova
> che 'l dito alla moglier ha ne la fica.
> Questo annel tenga in dito, e non lo muova
> mai chi non vuol ricevere vergogna
> da la sua donna; e a pena anco gli giova,
> pur ch'ella voglia, e farlo si dispogna.
> [Ariosto, Satira V 319-328]

Subsequently the story was related several times in prose and verse, in French, English and Latin; the best-known version is by Lafontaine, 'L'anneau de Hans Carvel. Conte tiré de

view, in the closing lines of *The Merchant of Venice*, which would seem fairly banal without such a joke. After the conversation has already become somewhat lewd, Gratiano says, undoubtedly with the same meaning as in Rabelais:

> Well, while I live I'll fear no other thing
> So sore as keeping safe Nerissa's ring.
>   (*The Merchant of Venice* 5.1.305-306)

Similarly, Rabelais has:

> if thou wilt believe me, in imitation of this example, never fail to have continually the ring of thy wife's commodity upon thy finger.
>   (Vol. 2, p. 142)

> A cestuy exemple foys, si me croys, que continuellement tu ayes l'anneau de ta femme on doigt.
>   (Esmangart, vol. 5, p. 40)

Rabelais also clearly provided Iago's expression 'the beast with two backs' (*Othello* 1.1.118), which is widespread in France today, and may have been earlier, but is only ever traced back to Rabelais, who uses it twice (Book 1, chapter 3, and Book 5,

---

Rabelais'. Because of Rabelais's choice of name, though with no stronger evidence, the joke has been ascribed a German origin and connected to a jest-book by a German, *Mensa philosophica*, available in editions dated 1489, 1577, 1588, 1602 and 1608 (cf. Regis, vol. 2, p. 426; Esmangart, vol. 5, p. 25).

chapter 31).[29] Finally, Rabelais jokes about girls 'falling backwards' (Book 5, chapter 21) in the same spirit as the Nurse in *Romeo and Juliet* (1.3.44).

6. Among the curious comparisons common to both writers, we must mention that with Jack of the clock, a bronze figure who struck the hour on great clocks. This comparison is made by Rabelais (Book 1, chapter 2, and in the new prologue to Book 4) in the same way as in *Timon of Athens* (3.7.89 ['minute-jacks']), *Richard II* (5.5.60 ['jack of the clock']) and *Richard III* (4.2.117 ['like a jack, thou keep'st the stroke']). Similarly, we can compare the mention of bowling as a term of 'neighbourly' praise in Rabelais and Shakespeare:

> all stiffe drinkers, brave fellows, and good players at the kyles
>   (Book 1, chapter 4; vol. 1, p. 17)

> tous bons beuveurs, bons compaignons, et beaulx joueurs de quille da
>   (Esmangart, vol. 1, p. 116)

> He is a marvellous good neighbour, faith, and a very good bowler
>   (*Love's Labour's Lost* 5.2.572-573)

---

[29] See Esmangart, vol. 1, pp. 104-105 [for a rather peculiar footnote on this].

In the same scene the ugly, meagre face of the schoolmaster Holofernes is compared with the carved wooden face on the neck of a zither, a comparison that occurs in Rabelais (Book 2, chapter 3).[30] Rabelais also has the name Holofernes for a similar personality, for in Book 1, chapter 14 he mentions 'a great Sophister-Doctor, called Master Tubal Holofernes' (vol. 1, p. 46), who has been identified with various learned pedants of the day.[31] From this source in Rabelais Shakespeare must have transferred the name Holofernes to his comedy, and the name Tubal to *The Merchant of Venice*.[32]

7. A peculiar word occurring in both writers is 'hurly-burly', which in Shakespeare means the tumult of war (*Macbeth* 1.1.3; *1 Henry IV* 5.1.78) and in Rabelais, with a similar sense, refers to people (Book 5, prologue [mon grand Hurluburlu; Esmangart, vol. 7, p. 221] and chapter 15 [sainct Hurluburlu, pp. 415-416]). However, Shakespeare probably took it from Peacham's *Garden of Eloquence* (1577), where it is explained, corresponding

---

[30] Car elle avoyt visaige de rebec (Esmangart, vol. 3, p. 111).
[31] [U]n grand docteur sophiste nommé Thubal-Holoferne (Esmangart, vol. 1, p. 269); also p. 276: ung grand docteur sophiste, nomme maistre Thubal Holoferne.
[32] The name does occur in the Bible, but only as a geographical name in Isaiah 66:19, besides, of course, Tubalcain in Genesis.

to his usage, as 'uproar and tumultuous stir'.[33]

8. Among proverbial terms and expressions with a more or less superstitious basis, we find in both writers references to the right limb as the better and more fortunate (Rabelais, Book 1, chapter 25; *Titus Andronicus* 2.3.192; *King John* 4.2.170), along with the fabulous unicorn and the longevity of crows (*Gargantua and Pantagruel*, Book 5, prologue; *The Phoenix and the Turtle* 17: 'And thou treble-dated crow').[34]

Finally, a play on words must be mentioned for which Rabelais and Shakespeare use the word *salade* (English 'sallet') in the same way, meaning both a helmet and the familiar vegetable.[35]

---

[33] Cf. Regis, vol. 2, p. 766; Delius *ad Macbeth* 1.1.3; Esmangart, vol. 7, pp. 221-222n.

[34] The ancients believed that the crow lived nine times as long as a human being: Ovid, *Metamorphoses* 7.274; Pliny, *Historia Naturalis* 7.48.

[35] Rabelais, Book 4, chapter 29: Les aliments desquels il se paist, sont aubers sallez, casquets, morions sallez, et salades sallees' (vol. 6, p. 274) ['His usual food is pickled coats of mail, salt helmets and head-pieces, and salt sallads' (vol. 3, p. 19)]. Cf. *2 Henry VI* 4.9.5-13:

> ... Wherefore o'er a brick wall have I climbed into this garden to see if I can eat grass or pick a sallet another while, which is not amiss to cool a man's stomach this

Many more individual resemblances could perhaps be added to those already mentioned, but what has been cited so far sufficiently licenses the conclusion concerning the extent and nature of Shakespeare's inspiration through Rabelais. Only one further passage shall be mentioned, since it appears to have influenced Portia's well-known speech about mercy, which we shall also compare with other passages. Here, therefore, are the relevant lines from *The Merchant of Venice* (4.1.179-192):

> The quality of mercy is not strained.
> It droppeth as the gentle rain from heaven
> Upon the place beneath. It is twice blest:
> It blesseth him that gives, and him that takes.
> 'Tis mightiest in the mightiest. It becomes
> The thronèd monarch better than his crown.
> His sceptre shows the force of temporal power,
> The attribute to awe and majesty,
> Wherein doth sit the dread and fear of kings;
> But mercy is above this sceptred sway.
> It is enthronèd in the hearts of kings;
> It is an attribute to God himself,
> And earthly power doth then show likest God's
> When mercy seasons justice.

---

hot weather. And I think this word 'sallet' was born to do me good; for many a time, but for a sallet, my brain-pan had been cleft with a brown bill; and many a time, when I have been dry, and bravely marching, it hath served me instead of a quart pot to drink in; and now the word 'sallet' must serve me to feed on.

In his edition, Schlegel omits the entire passage based on the wordplay, considering it untranslatable.

The third and fourth of these lines can be traced back to the following passage from Rabelais (Book 4, chapter 4):

> ... the sentence of the Stoicks, who say, that there are three parts in a benefit, the one of the giver, the other of the receiver, the third of the remunerator; and that the receiver rewards the giver when he freely receives the benefit, and always remembers it; as on the contrary, that man is most ungrateful who despises and forgets a benefit.
> (Vol. 2, p. 280)

> ... par la sentence des stoïciens: lesquels disoyent trois parties estre en benefice. L'une du donnant, l'aultre du recepvant, la tierce du recompensant: et le recepvant tres bien recompenser le donnant, quand il accepte voluntiers le bienfaict, et le retient en soubvenance perpetuelle: comme au rebours le recepvant estre le plus ingrat du monde, qui mepriseroyt et oublieroyt le benefice.
> (Esmangart, vol. 5, p. 507)

Rabelais's authority for this Stoic view is obviously Seneca, whose *De Beneficiis* contains much the same sentiment.[36] Hence Shakespeare could also have been prompted by the latter, but it is surely more probable that he had Rabelais in mind.

---

[36] ... quare tres Gratiae et quare sorores sint, et quare manibus implexis, et quare ridentes et iuvenes et virgines solutaque ac perlucida veste. Alii quidem videri volunt unam esse, quae det beneficium, alteram, quae accipiat, tertiam, quae reddat; alii tria beneficorum esse genera, promerentium, reddentium, simul accipientium reddentiumque (Seneca, *De Beneficiis* 1.3.2-3); reddit enim beneficium, qui debet (1.1.3-4).

[The list of analogues and antecedents for the 'Quality of mercy' speech from *The Merchant of Venice* continues in the next chapter, where it introduces König's discussion of Italian playwrights.]

Chapter Two

Shakespeare and Some Italian Dramatists

[Picking up our discussion again from the 'Quality of mercy' speech in *The Merchant of Venice* (4.1.179-192),] the poetic expression 'It droppeth as the gentle rain from heaven' (180) is modelled on the following passage from the Bible, a text that undoubtedly had a considerable influence on Shakespeare's poetic language:

> My doctrine shall drop as the rain, my speech shall distil as the dew, as the small rain upon the tender herb, and as the showers upon the grass.
> (Deut. 32:2 KJV)

Greene too has a similar expression in *Friar Bacon and Friar Bungay*:

> Sins have their salves, repentance can do much:
> Think mercy sits where Justice holds her seat,
> And from those wounds those bloody Jews did pierce,[41]

---

[41] [In quoting this passage in German translation, König replaces what follows the first half of this line with an *omissis* sign. We quote the full passage because this is obviously relevant to the plot of the *Merchant of Venice*, and the idea of Antonio as a Christ-like figure (and in a comedy at that) is a rather powerful one, which deserves to be explored, also in relation to his namesakes in other Shakespearean plays. On the other hand, the last three lines quoted here resonate with the

> Which by thy magic oft did bleed afresh,
> From thence for thee the dew of mercy drops.
>   (H1r)

The idea that mercy raises us to the level of the gods is found earlier in *Titus Andronicus*.[42] It is also formulated as early as Cicero,[43] and in essence also in *Don Quixote*.[44] Much more similar, however, is the following passage from the tragedy *Rodopeia* by Leonoro Verlato, which also provided the main

---

ending of Marlowe's *Dr Faustus* – 'See, see, where Christ's blood streams in the firmament | One drop would save my soul, half a drop', etc.]

[42] 1.1.117-119: 'Wilt thou draw near the nature of the gods? | Draw near them then in being merciful. | Sweet mercy is nobility's true badge.' In *Richard II*, too (5.3.109-134), the praises of mercy are sung; and the closest resemblance to Portia's speech is in Isabella's words in *Measure for Measure* (2.2.61-65):

> No ceremony that to great ones 'longs,
> Not the king's crown, nor the deputed sword,
> The marshal's truncheon, nor the judge's robe,
> Become them with one half so good a grace
> As mercy does.

[43] *Pro Ligario* 12, 38: Homines enim ad deos nulla re propius accedunt quam salutem hominibus dando.

[44] The instructions that Don Quixote gives to Sancho Panza when the latter is about to enter on his governorship include this: 'In the trial of criminals, consider as much as thou canst without prejudice to the plaintiff, how defenceless and open the miserable are to the temptations of our corrupt and depraved nature, and so far show thyself full of pity and clemency; for though God's attributes are equal, yet his mercy is more attractive and pleasing in our eyes, than his justice.' (Part 2, chapter 42; vol. 4, p. 59).

outline of Portia's speech.[45] The tragic or rather would-be tragic substance of the play is the cruelty of a father, King Ismaro of Thrace, to his daughter Rodopeia, to whom he sends the heart and liver of her lover, the Prince of Armenia, having had him killed simply because the Prince carried on an amorous relationship with the Princess in the guise of a gardener's boy. Before the murder is performed, the King's confidant Arsete seeks to dissuade him from it and to encourage forgiveness, as follows:

> Thus let me say that since the King of Thrace is celebrated and admired the world over as a fierceless lord, he can never be held a coward for granting this

---

[45] The tragedy appeared at Venice in 1582 and so could well have been available to Shakespeare. The passage quoted reveals that although the Italian poet writes in a mellifluous and accomplished style, in some places with Dante as an obvious model, he thought the art of tragedy lay in hair-raising effects. As a curiosity, it may also be mentioned that the Prince is slaughtered and has his heart torn out in full view of the audience, and the murderer, who describes himself as the King's personal bandit, so to speak, declares his pleasure at the sight of the beautiful torn-out heart:

> Tenete aperta ben questa ferita,
> Ch'io gli voglio levar dal petto il core.
> Ecco l'ho sradicato: oh, che bel core.
>
> (*Rodopeia* 4.6, 54r)

This has a counterpart in the heart-rending conversations that the Princess later carries on with the torn-out heart, held in her hand. The unnatural murder and the murder scene have left no trace in any of the scenes where Shakespeare presents murderers, and which could scarcely have been drawn from life – another instance confirming that he borrowed only what he found usable and viable.

magnanimous pardon. In fact, he will be praised for his mercy. Among great souls this praise never grows stale, as is the way with worldly honours and that fame that comes from great enterprises, or from the uncertain fortunes of war: that honour is soon forgotten, which fortune bestows upon many. Mercy alone is that virtue through which man raises himself on a par with God.

> Per questo io voglio dir, ch'essendo omai
> Riverito dal mondo, e conosciuto
> Il Re di Tracia per signore invitto,
> Non puote conseguir nome di vile
> Con questo sì magnanimo perdono,
> Ma degnissima laude di clemente:
> Lode, ch'appresso i generosi spirti
> Non invecchia giammai, come gli onori,
> E' pregi conseguiti da le imprese,
> E da' perigli de le incerte guerre:
> Che facilmente quell'onor s'oblia,
> Che da fortuna è compartito a molti;
> Ma la clemenzia è quella virtù sola,
> In cui pur l'uomo si pareggia a Dio
>   (*Rodopeia* 4.4, 50r-v)

Nor is the passage just quoted the only one in the Italian tragedy to display similarities to Shakespeare. In Act 5, scene 6 (73v), there occurs the line:

> No more words, no: it is time to resort to deeds
> Non più parole, no, la man s'adopre

in which we recognize the less colourful model for Casca's exclamation at the murder of Julius Caesar:

> Speak, hands, for me![46]
> (*Julius Caesar* 3.1.76)

We must also notice a long reflective speech addressed by the gardener Serinda to Sinibaldo, whom she loves in vain, since he is in love with the Princess (beginning of Act 3); she mentions the same rising scale of happiness that occurs in another beautiful speech by Portia in Act 3, scene 2. Serinda begins by praising in general terms the happiness of those who inspire love, especially in such a handsome prince as she has before her; still happier are those who can also embrace their beloved. She then says that she too is happy after a fashion in having brought such a comely couple together; she would be even happier if her beloved perceived the fire of love consuming her, and happiest of all if he returned it and, as she puts it, cooled it to the right temperature.[47]

---

[46] The first murderer in *Richard III* (1.3.349-350) utters similar words: 'Talkers are no good doers. Be assured, | We go to use our hands, and not our tongues.'

[47] Cf. *Rodopeia* 3.1, 23v:

> Ma ben felice lei, che in questo stato
> Fa con la sua beltà vivere amante
> Prencipe così degno, e così bello:
> E più felice allor, ch'entro le braccia
> Sì bel pegno d'amor contenta accoglie.
> Felice quasi, e fortunata anch'io,
> Che fui mezzo, e cagion de' primi amori,
> E poi d'unir sì bella coppia insieme,
> Che sentia incenerirsi a poco a poco
> Di fiamme ardenti l'amoroso seno.

Portia, addressing her Bassanio, says, admittedly with better motivation, that she is likewise happy:

> Happy in this, she is not yet so old
> But she may learn; happier than this,
> She is not bred so dull but she can learn;
> Happiest of all is that her gentle spirit
> Commits itself to yours to be directed
> As from her lord, her governor, her king.
> (*The Merchant of Venice* 3.2.160-165)

One of the better parts of the Italian tragedy is the chorus that closes the fourth act (following the slaughter of the Prince, as described above), and which often resonates with views found in Shakespeare, as well as showing individual similarities of expression with Shakespearean lines. What makes it particularly interesting is that it often corresponds to reflections uttered by Hamlet, thus confirming our assumption, especially with reference to the other similarities demonstrated here, that Shakespeare had this chorus to hand while writing more than one work. The material he took from it, however, he used with such accomplished freedom, pithy brevity and poetic vigour that the similarity is not marked. To permit a comparison,

---

> Ma più felice, s'un incendio tale,
> Ch'arde (misera me) tutto 'l mio petto,
> Fosse palese al mio Signore amato:
> E 'n fine felicissima, se poi
> Conosciuto l'ardor di tanto foco,
> Volesse con pietà tepido farlo.

we must quote almost the whole of the rather long chorus:[48]

> [1] Mother Nature, the highest and first cause, after she set every thing in order with great providence and mastery and situated the elements in their appropriate place here and there, took merciful care to adorn the earth with a thousand beautiful things. On this emisphere she shaped man, worthiest of creatures, with art and thought, and with his face uplifted in contemplation of the stars.[[49]] In his specific form, she showed her own nourishing image.
>
> [14] Adorned with the image of God, the most perfect and sacred on the surface of the earth, man stood above all other mortal creatures. With his venerable face lifted up to the highest Heaven and the eternal Maker, in order that he should be all the more grateful and pious towards Him, man ruled over the other animals, and was given knowledge of immortal things through his inner value. This infused his heart with the sacred desire and devout aspiration to become a citizen of Heaven.
>
> [28] And this is how it happens: after triumphing over every base appetite, reason rises from the senses to intellect in an almost angelical manner. There it feeds on Good that is perfect to a degree far above anything that is not found on earth, and which is worthy not only of the highest admiration but of being worshipped as divine by all people. Oh happy he who, from the moment that he is born, carries in him such a worth source of eternal honour. But woe to him who forgets

---

[48] Except for the last three stanzas, which refer to the play in a way that is not of interest here.

[49] [This stanza is closely related to the beginning of Ovid's *Metamorphoses*. With this sentence in particular, cf. *Metamorphoses* 1.85-86: 'os homini sublime dedit caelumque videre | iussit et erectos ad sidera tollere vultus'.]

that he is made in such way that he can make himself noble, and as if he were immortal.

⁴² Alas, unhappy world, how seldom does man indeed think and exert himself to lift his reason up from his senses to his Heaven-given intellect, and apply to that purpose that is worthy of him. Instead, he gives himself up to his insane appetite. He becomes cruel, proud and irascible: as if he were an animal, devoid of that good, which man is sometimes given in vain. So far is he encumbered by the earthly weight that encloses his soul, that often his senses triumph over his reason.

⁵⁶ Thus he gives free rein to pride, ire, the most unchecked desires, hideous lust, cruel envy. Thus he foolishly goes wherever his appetite seems to call him, and he can be seen to be swept along in pursuit of that fallacious good that base people admire. Thus is the world filled all over with poison. And because of this, those nourishing virtues, whom every noble spirit amongst us in this vile cloister yearn to see, are fled to the highest heavens.

> L'alta e prima cagion madre natura,
> Poi che tutte le cose con ordine dispose,
> Con tanta provvidenzia e magistero,
> E ch'al suo luogo gli elementi pose
> E 'n queste parti e 'n quelle   5
> Da mille cose belle
> D'ornar la terra ebbe pietosa cura.
> Formò d'arte e pensiero
> Sopra questo emisfero
> Col volto eretto a contemplar le stelle   10
> L'uom degno più d'ogn'altra creatura,
> Nella cui forma espressa
> Mostrò l'alma sembianza di se stessa.
> Ornato dell'immagine di Dio
> Più perfetto e più santo   15
> Sopra il terrestre manto,
> Tutti l'uom superò gli altri mortali:

E con l'aspetto venerabil tanto
Alzato al Ciel superno
Verso il Fattore eterno,   20
Perché fosse ver lui più grato e pio
Resse gli altri animali
E le cose immortali
Conobbe ancor col suo valore interno;
Che gl'infuse nel cor santo desio   25
Col più devoto zelo
Di poter farsi Cittadin del Cielo.
E così avvien, s'eleva la ragione
(Vinto ogni basso affetto)
Da' sensi all'intelletto,   30
Quasi angelicamente, onde si pasce
Sopra l'uso mondan di ben perfetto:
Non pur d'alto stupore
Degno, ma che si adore,
Come divin, da tutte le persone.   35
O felice chi nasce,
E porta dalle fasce
Così degna cagion d'eterno onore;
Ma misero colui, ch'in oblio pone
D'esser fattura tale,   40
Che può farsi gentil, come immortale.
Ahi, che di rado avvien, misero mondo,
Che l'uom discorra, o pensi
Trar la ragion da' sensi
All'intelletto, che dal Ciel gli viene,   45
Per scorgerlo a quel fin, ch'a lui conviensi:
Ch'anzi si dona in mano
All'appetito insano,
E crudele, e superbo, e iracondo,
Quasi animal diviene,   50
Che manchi di quel bene,
Ch'all'uom'è dato alcuna volta invano;
Così l'aggrava il suo terreno pondo,
Da cui l'anima è cinta,
Ch'è spesso la ragion da' sensi vinta.   55
Quindi si allenta alla superbia, all'ira,
Alle più ingorde brame,

> Alla lussuria infame,
> All'invidia crudel libero il freno.
> Quindi ove par, che l'appetito il chiame   60
> L'uom move incauto il piede,
> E trasportar si vede
> Dietro il fallace ben, che 'l volgo ammira:
> Quindi è sparso, e ripieno
> Il mondo di veleno: 65
> Quindi volaro alla superna sede
> L'alme virtù, che di veder sospira
> In questo chiostro vile
> Ogni animo tra noi fatto gentile.
>   (*Rodopeia* 4, Chorus, 54v-56r)

Hamlet's words containing the clearest echoes of this chorus are as follows. First in Act 2, scene 2 (293-298), after speaking of earth, air and fire:

> What a piece of work is a man! How noble in reason, how infinite in faculty, in form and moving how express and admirable, in action how like an angel, in apprehension how like a god – the beauty of the world, the paragon of animals! And yet to me what is this quintessence of dust?

Then at 4.4.23-29:

>   What is a man
> If his chief good and market of his time
> Be but to sleep and feed? – a beast, no more.
> Sure, he that made us with such large discourse,
> Looking before and after, gave us not
> That capability and god-like reason
> To fust in us unused.

Moreover, the idea of the earthy enclosure that occurs twice in the *Rodopeia* chorus (at lines 53-54 and 68),[50] must have given rise to the similar expression in *The Merchant of Venice* (5.1.63-64):

> But whilst this muddy vesture of decay
> Doth grossly close it in, we cannot hear it.

The last words of the chorus quoted above (66-67) likewise occasioned the following words in *Venus and Adonis* (ll. 793-794):

> Call it not love, for love to heaven is fled
> Since sweating lust on earth usurped his name.

Finally we must mention the chorus that concludes the entire tragedy, and therewith take our leave of this work. In some places, in the opening and closing lines, it resembles the following passage from *Richard III* (3.4.96-101):

> O momentary grace of mortal men,
> Which we more hunt for than the grace of God.
> Who builds his hope in th'air of your good looks
> Lives like a drunken sailor on a mast,
> Ready with every nod to tumble down
> Into the fatal bowels of the deep.

However, it is uncertain whether the resemblance is accidental or the consequence of imitation. If the latter is the case, it is interesting to observe the freedom with which the poet applied the same expressions and images to a quite different train of

---

[50] See also in the third last stanza, which we have not quoted: Il più bel pregio offese, | Che mai venisse da Natura in sorte | A vestirsi tra noi di carnal panno (*Rodopeia*, 56r, ll. 79-81).

thought. The lines from *Rodopeia* that invite comparison are the following [i.e. the final lines of the play]:

> O vain hopes of mortal men! In this tempestuous sea of life ... if the ship is suddenly rocked by a storm ... then the helmsman turns all pale with fear. In the end, everyone comes to recognize that, from the moment of their birth, they carry with them rain, storms, tempests and winds that mean to shipwreck them: in vain would they hope to find in such wintry weather that Good that only resides in the lap of the eternal Mover.

> O speranze fallaci di mortali.
> Questo di vita tempestoso mare
> ...
> Ma se nova procella il legno fiede
> ...
> Rende il dubbio nocchier pallido e smorto:
> Ch'alfin diviene accorto
> Ogn'un, quando egli nasce
> Seco addur da le fasce
> Piogge, fortune, tempestati e venti
> Al suo naufragio intenti,
> E che speranza vanamente il pasce,
> Se trovar crede in così orribil verno
> Il ben ch'è in grembo del Motore eterno.

Before turning to another Italian play and the use Shakespeare made of it, let us return to the passage from Cicero, quoted above, to which we did not trace back similar words of Shakespeare's, and to prove that he was also familiar with this writer, a model of classical Latin, quote another passage which in our view Shakespeare appropriated in a noteworthy manner. In Cicero's *De Oratore* we find (3.41):

> I deprecate the expression that the death of Africanus 'left the state gelt', or that Glaucia was 'the excrement of the House of Lords'.
>
> Nolo dici morte Africani 'castratam' esse rempublicam, nolo 'stercus curiae' dici Glauciam.

The rather peculiar images found here are repeated in *Henry VI* by the rebel Jack Cade at two different but adjacent places, namely:

> I tell you that that Lord Saye hath gelded the commonwealth, and made it an eunuch.
> (*2 Henry VI* 4.2.149-150)

and

> Be it known unto thee ... that I am the besom that must sweep the court clean of such filth as thou art.
> (4.7.24-27)

Here it must be emphasized that neither of these passages appears in the old play *Henry VI*, although in the aforementioned scenes Cade's speeches are otherwise almost identical in the new and the old play. Hence it is quite evident that Shakespeare, who, as mentioned earlier, was responsible also for the old *Henry VI*, had, between writing the first and the second version, read or re-read the aforementioned book by Cicero, and that this passage struck him as suitable to provide an original embellishment for the speeches of his Jack Cade.[51]

Finally, we shall turn to another little-known product of Italian literature, in order to demonstrate that it supplied the model for many details in one of the most famous passages in Shakespeare. This is Hamlet's discourse on the nature of drama, and it is worth examining the likely sources, even if they were used only casually. Hamlet says:

> let them [the actors] be well used, for they are the abstracts and brief chronicles of the time.
> (*Hamlet* 2.2.503-504)

> For anything so overdone is from the purpose of playing, whose end, both at the first and now, was and is to hold as 'twere the mirror up to nature: to show virtue her own feature, scorn her own image, and the very age and body of the time his form and pressure. Now, this overdone, or come tardy off, though it make the unskilful laugh, cannot but make the judicious grieve; the censure of the which one must in your allowance o'erweigh a whole theatre of others.
> (*Hamlet* 3.2.18-25)

The model for this is found in the prelude to the comedy *The Witch* (*La strega*) by Antonio

---

[51] This is assuming that the Quarto editions [entitled *The First Part of the Contention of the Two Famous Houses of York and Lancaster*] were previous redactions, rather than simply mangled versions, of the play in question; see the Introduction to *Henry VI* in Ulrici's edition of the works of Shakespeare (with the Schlegel-Tieck translation) published by the Deutsche Shakespeare-Gesellschaft (vol. 3, pp. 22ff).

Francesco Grazzini, a founding member of the Academy of the 'Damp' (*Umidi*), and later of the Accademia della Crusca in Florence.[52] As a member of the former he assumed the name Lasca (a freshwater fish), by which he is usually known. He lived from 1503 to 1583 [or 1584], and several of his comedies were printed at Venice in 1582.[53] Hence they must have been available to Shakespeare, albeit only in the original.[54] This would prove, as does the example of *Rodopeia*, that Shakespeare knew Italian. In the aforementioned prelude, Prologo and Argomento carry on a conversation about the purpose and requirements of comedy, with Prologo representing the demands of art, Argomento those of current taste. The former exclaims:

> ... don't you know that comedies are images of truth, examples of customs and a mirror of life?
>
> ... non sai tu che le commedie sono immagini di verità, esempio di costumi e specchio di vita?
>
> (*La strega*, 'Interlocutori nel principio', 7r)

---

[52] [König's discussion of Antonfrancesco Grazzini's *La strega* is reprised in Elisabetta Tarantino, 'Shakespeare and Religious War: New Developments on the Italian Sources of *Twelfth Night*', *Shakespeare Survey* 72 (2019): 32-47 (on pp. 41-42).]

[53] [In his footnote here König refers to the text of *La strega* in *Teatro classico italiano* (Leipzig: Fleicher, 1829). We quote, in modernized form, from the 1582 Giunti edition, which is available on Google Books. *La strega* translations are ours, pending a facing-page edition currently in preparation.]

[54] [For some preliminary information on the fortune of Grazzini in Shakespeare's England, see Tarantino, 'Shakespeare and Religious War', pp. 40-42.]

In reply to this, Argomento maintains that the only purpose of comedies is to entertain and to drive away melancholy, further pointing out that the theatre should keep pace with the times. Prologo, however, insists that those authors who are blessed with learning and understanding fit their plots to a higher artistic purpose, rather than the other way round, and rebuts Argomento's unflattering description of their supposed 'mishmash' of ancient and modern. The discussion continues as follows:

> ARGUMENT These ladies have come here to relax and to enjoy themselves, but you would like them to be astonished and confused, hearing a pedantic little fable, that sounds like a sermon or like a speech that would not make anyone else either laugh or cry.
> PROLOGUE These valiant men would be satisfied recognizing in it the comic art and the rules of comedy.
> ARGUMENT You are very young: these valiant men have not come here to see and hear the comedy.
> PROLOGUE Well why have they come here?
> ARGUMENT In order to see and contemplate the immense beauty, the exquisite charm, the divine grace of these most noble and honest young women, damsels and ladies, so that the comedy will not be visible to their eyes, or audible to their ears.
> PROLOGUE In the name of God, I would always want to go along with the opinion of those who are learned and wise.
>
> ARGOMENTO Tu vorresti che quelle gentildonne, che son venute per ricrearsi e rallegrarsi, stessero attonite e confuse udendo una favoluccia pedantesca che tenesse di predica o di sermone, da non fare altrui né ridere né piagnere.

PROLOGO Questi valent'uomini restarebbero soddisfatti loro riconoscendo in quella l'arte e i precetti comici.
ARGOMENTO Tu sei bene giovane: questi valent'uomini non sono venuti qui per vedere e udire la commedia.
PROLOGO O perché ci sono venuti?
ARGOMENTO Per vedere e contemplare la immensa bellezza, la somma leggiadria, la divina grazia di queste nobilissime e onestissime giovani donne, madonne e signore; di maniera che la commedia passerà invisibile a gl'occhi e a gl'orecchi loro.
PROLOGO Al nome di Dio, io vorrei sempre andarmene con l'opinione di coloro che sanno.

(*La strega*, 'Interlocutori nel principio', 8r-v)

The general meaning of the prologue is the subject of a discussion in Lasca that resembles the one in *Hamlet*. Soon after the beginning of the prelude, Prologo expresses himself as follows:

> ... which is why in the opening scenes of the first act the best writers bring onstage some characters who, through their dialogue, open and reveal to the audience everything that has taken place before and part of what will take place afterwards in the comedy.
>
> ... perciocché nelle prime scene del primo atto s'introducono, dai componitori migliori, alcuni personaggi che per via di ragionamento aprono e manifestano agli uditori tutto quello che è seguito innanzi e parte di quello che deve seguir dopo nella commedia.
>
> (*La strega*, 'Interlocutori nel principio', 5r)

In *Hamlet*, at the beginning of the dumb show, Ophelia says: 'Belike this show imports the argument of the play' (3.2.126). Then, on the entry of the Prologue:

HAMLET We shall know by this fellow. The players cannot keep counsel, they'll tell all.
OPHELIA Will a tell us what this show meant?
HAMLET Ay ...
   (*Hamlet* 3.2.127-130)

The content of this last passage is not important, but it is noteworthy inasmuch as it confirms that the poet deliberately incorporated his views on dramatic art, only in outline yet with a certain completeness, into this, his most profound and mature tragedy.[55]

---

[55] Hamlet's observations on the nature of drama have a parallel in later Italian literature which is even more strikingly similar than those quoted above. It may be mentioned here because it proves either that Shakespeare was known to the Italian poets even at a time when he was neither correctly understood nor widely appreciated, or that such different poets as Shakespeare and Goldoni – for it is he of whom we are speaking – expressed the same ideas in the same manner. Both, of course, were intimately familiar with the stage, so it is natural for them to draw up the same rules as the result of their views. In Goldoni's comedy *Teatro comico*, which has as its subject the activity on stage when a comedy is being rehearsed, we find (Act 3, scene 3):

> Guardatevi sopra tutto dalla cantilena, e dalla declamazione, ma recitate naturalmente, come se parlaste, mentre, essendo la commedia una imitazione della natura, si deve fare tutto quello che è verisimile. Circa al gesto, anche questo deve essere naturale. Movete le mani secondo il senso della parola. [cf. *Hamlet* 3.2.4-5: 'Nor do not saw the air too much with your hand, thus, but use all gently'; 16-17: 'Suit the action to the word, the word to the action'. (König's remark)] Gestite per lo più colla dritta, e poche volte colla sinistra, e avvertite di non moverle tutte due in una volta, se non quando un impeto di collera, una sorpresa, una esclamazione lo richiedesse; servendovi di regola,

Our assumption that the resemblance between the quoted passages is not coincidental gains additional plausibility from the fact that Grazzini's play also contains yet another passage that Shakespeare has clearly imitated in the following words of Portia's:

> How oddly he is suited! I think he bought his doublet in Italy, his round hose in France, his bonnet in Germany, and his behaviour everywhere.
> (*The Merchant of Venice* 1.2.61-64)

Compare the following dialogue in Grazzini:

> TADDEO What are they laughing at, then?
> FARFANICCHIO They are laughing at the strange clothes that you are wearing.
> TADDEO Why, are my clothes so very odd?
> FARFANICCHIO Extremely odd. You are – forgive me: Your Lordship is – wearing a German bonnet, a French cape, a Florentine gown, a Spanish ruff, Gascony stockings, Roman shoes, a Fiesole face, a Sienese brain, and a jennet plume. Do you not call this odd?
>
> TADDEO O di che diavol ride [la gente]?
> FARFANICCHIO Ride dell'abito stravagante che voi avete indosso.
> TADDEO O è egli però abito sì stravagante questo?

> che principiando il periodo con una mano, mai non si finisce coll'altra, ma con quella con cui si principia, terminare ancora si deve.

See also Act 3, scene 11:

> L'Arlecchino deve parlar poco, ma a tempo. Deve dire la sua botta frizzante, e non stiracchiata.

> FARFANICCHIO Stravagantissimo. Voi avete, cioè la Signoria Vostra ha la berretta alla tedesca, la cappa alla franzese, il saione alla fiorentina, il colletto sòpravi alla spagnuola, le calze alla guascona, le scarpette alla romanesca, il viso alla fiesolana, il cervello alla sanese e lo spennacchio alla giannetta: non vi pare stravaganza questa?
>
> (*La strega* 3.1, 19r)

The examples cited so far would suffice to represent the very diverse ways in which Shakespeare adapted the words and creations of others for whatever his own work demanded. Our admiration for him is not diminished, but rather increased, since as a rule we will thus recognize and observe in him, in small as well as in more significant matters, the same artistry, the same just perception and the same poetic genius that is revealed throughout his creations. One may take him to task for sometimes choosing unsuitable materials for poetic adaptation, but for the most part he makes ample amends by the way he does it, by the subtle elaboration to which he submits his materials, and the beautiful manner in which he shapes them. And if we go back to the essence of poetry, to the inmost source of poetic creation, no poet can ever be criticized for his choice of subject-matter, unless indeed it revealed a vulgar mind, and then we would not be dealing with a true poet. It is only the literary artisan who makes a rational choice of materials and can work on them at any time, whereas the poet's achievements must proceed from an inner urge, and if this is not the case, he can hardly achieve anything first-rate. So the material must appeal to the poet, rather than the poet searching for the material, and this was always the case with Shakespeare, though he no doubt also read voraciously in order to find material that might appeal to him.[56]

If, as we have seen, Shakespeare absorbed into his works much of greater or less significance, indeed much that was trivial, found in the writings of others; if he transplanted into his rich poetic garden many a forgotten flower that he saw blooming beside his path; if he picked up many building-blocks from the poetic rubble of literature and restored their brilliance and dignity by fitting them into the sublime edifice of his work; we can regard this neither as a sign of poetic weakness, nor as an unjustified seizure of others' intellectual property, nor, putting it mildly, as an impertinent grasping of what was available to all. On the contrary, we see in this an expression of that modesty which we would gladly consider a principal trait in the enigmatic character of this great poet, shown in his refraining from creating something new where prior materials could properly be used and were still waiting for poetic treatment. The objection might indeed be raised that such a mighty

---

[56] Shakespeare would also have been influenced by his audience and his position in the theatre: on this subject, see, by the present author, *Shakespeare als Dichter, Weltweiser und Christ. Durch Erläuterung von Vier seiner Dramen und eine Vergleichung mit Dante dargestellt* (Leipzig, 1873), pp. 56ff.

spirit as Shakespeare could have achieved something better if he had invented the subject-matter of his works out of whole cloth. However, besides a certain reverence for the prior materials which he preserved, he must often have been guided by the awareness that he could achieve more by working on a prior basis and expending all his strength on creating a solid structure, than by making it his task to shape the phantoms of his imagination and thus erect an unsteady building on an equally unsteady foundation. He may well have found it more rewarding to approach already existing materials with his steadfast judgement, making them intelligible, animating them, and turning them into a rounded whole, than to wrestle from the outset with his imagination and perhaps to be led thereby beyond the limits of his sound judgement. Therein he resembled the great Greek tragedians, who for the most part invented nothing, but celebrated their ancestral myths and traditions, enabling them to live for eternity.

Chapter Three

Shakespeare and Giordano Bruno

Shakespeare criticism is usually most at risk of going astray when it brings its poet and his works into a close connection with philosophy. Yet, although he certainly did not consider himself a philosopher, his profound understanding of human nature, especially of interacting and conflicting psychological forces, obliges us to regard him as a disciple and proponent of the branch of learning that is especially concerned with understanding the human mind and its relation to the world as a whole.[57] Of course, if this subject is considered only as the development of what is called a philosophical system, it is impossible to demonstrate that Shakespeare adhered to any particular system, or that he directly influenced the formation of such a system. Nonetheless, many disciples of philosophy,

---

[57] A comprehensive knowledge of philosophy is ascribed to Shakespeare e.g. by Hermann Marggraff in his work *W. Shakespeare als Lehrer der Menschheit* (Leipzig, 1864), where it is said: 'An English poetic autodidact, gifted by nature and educated merely by reading, cannot achieve such compositions as Shakespeare provided. Such lofty and wide-ranging poetry as Shakespeare's imperatively demands the most thorough knowledge and the deepest study of the greatest poetic creations of all previous ages. Shakespeare must likewise have had an intimate knowledge of all the philosophical systems that were known by then, for he reaches the highest philosophical standard of his age.'

both those who claim to be such and those whose search for understanding truly earns them the title, may well have found their philosophical understanding and development more enriched by Shakespeare's works than by the writings of many professional philosophers. To say how far Shakespeare himself was indebted to philosophical studies for his comprehensive understanding of human affairs depends on each individual's view of the relation – even more controversial in the past than at present – between his natural intuition and practical experience on one hand, and his schooling and studies on the other, in the production of his creative work. On this question, the most scrupulous inquiries have been undertaken, pursuing the most diverse directions and descending to the most minute details. Regarding the poet's philosophical education, the last word has not yet been said, and yet such inquiries are more important than trying to establish what Shakespeare knew about specific branches of learning such as medicine, law, etc. The subject-matter of philosophy is wide, indeed unlimited, and philosophy can be applied to every subject and to all knowledge. Hence, if such an inquiry is to demonstrate the traces of philosophical study in the poet's numerous works, on a large and a small scale, it must cover a broad and challenging field, and its findings, and its method of proof in individual cases, will be open to all manner of objections. However, since we consider such an inquiry likely to improve our understanding of the poet, let us try to make a contribution to this endeavour by disclosing the relation of Shakespeare's works to the contemporary philosopher Giordano Bruno. Shakespeare's commentators have hitherto devoted little attention to this topic, though recently Tschischwitz has earned gratitude by addressing it, albeit for the most part with reference only to *Hamlet*.[58]

An irrefutable proof that Shakespeare was no stranger to philosophical studies is that he not only owned Montaigne's *Essays*, but used it in his works.[59] This of course leaves entirely open the question whether he made an academic study of philosophy and whether he assigned much value to it. It has been argued, and Hebler, for example, has reinforced the argument by assembling many pertinent passages, that Shakespeare held a low

---

[58] Benno Tschischwitz, *Shakspere-Forschungen*, vol. 1: *Hamlet* (Halle, 1868); idem, *Shakspeare's Hamlet* (English text, with corrections and notes) (Halle, 1868). We shall not note every piece of evidence Tschischwitz has supplied. On the whole, he discusses most of the passages quoted here from *Hamlet* along the same lines as we do. [This important line of inquiry is surveyed and continued in Hilary Gatti, *The Renaissance Drama of Knowledge: Giordano Bruno in England* (London, 1989).]
[59] Montaigne provided the source for Gonzalo's 'commonwealth' speech in *The Tempest* (2.1.143-168). Cf. K. Elze, 'Die Abfassungszeit des Sturms', *Jahrbuch der Deutschen Shakespeare-Gesellschaft* 7 (1872): 29-47 (on p. 38), and König, 'Ueber die Entlehnungen Shakespeare's', p. 198 [now as chapter 1 above].

opinion of philosophy, since he generally draws attention to its deficiencies, not its strengths, and was anyway too much of a poet to be a philosopher.[60] We can concede the latter point only insofar as he was too much of a poet to pursue philosophy at the expense of his poetry, but we think that philosophical studies had a fruitful effect on his poetic creation and that in general he assigned to philosophy the value it deserves as a branch of learning. The passages suggesting otherwise cannot be discussed individually here, and Hebler does not allow individual passages to contradict his conclusion. We shall only permit ourselves some general observations, believing that due attention to them will lead to findings different from Hebler's.

In some of Shakespeare's earlier plays, *The Taming of the Shrew* and *Love's Labour's Lost*, young men anxious to devote themselves to the study of philosophy are presented in a manner obliging us to conclude that the poet found such studies congenial. If such studies are not mentioned in the further course of the plays, that lies in the nature of poetry, which cannot readily take philosophical or other study for its subject. Besides, in keeping with his deeply held convictions, the poet also came out against the immoderate and one-sided study of philosophy; this view is expressed in *The Taming of the Shrew* by the jokes made by the

---

[60] Cf. Carl Hebler, 'Shakespeare und die Philosophie', in his *Aufsätze über Shakespeare*, 2nd ed. (Bern, 1874), pp. 279-294.

young student Lucentio's servant, and in *Love's Labour's Lost* by Biron's poetic declamations and by the unfolding of the plot. It is true that later, in *Hamlet*, we see the other side of the coin, when philosophical speculation is shown as paralyzing the will, but the poet clearly wanted to present the hero as a man of outstanding intellectual abilities, and if he shows him to have had a philosophical training he is unmistakably linking philosophical study with high intelligence.

In a series of passages where philosophy is spoken of disparagingly or contemptuously, this is the expression of a passionate mood, as with Romeo, Constance in *King John* or Leonato in *Much Ado about Nothing*, and if the characters in the grip of strong emotion reject the consolations of philosophy, that proves nothing whatever. On the other hand, philosophical consolations have some effect on Claudio in *Measure for Measure* (3.1) and, though the effect may be short-lived, this is very far from proving that the poet despised philosophy in general. Indeed, a preference for philosophical reasoning could be inferred from the fact that here, as elsewhere, consolation is provided by philosophy and not by the Christian religion.

If elsewhere philosophy is treated humorously, indeed exposed to a kind of mockery, it must be borne in mind that in the scenes where his fools disport themselves Shakespeare introduces every possible subject as the target of puns and jests, while in the more serious parts of the plays, where passion rather than reflection speaks, there is much less room to talk seriously about serious matters. That is why much that can be exploited poetically in the garb of humour has no basis for serious dramatic treatment. Besides, the mockery that Shakespeare occasionally directs against philosophers and philosophy does not refer to learning as such, but to certain eccentricities in its treatment. Touchstone in *As You Like It*, in particular, delivers such attacks when he asks the shepherd if he knows anything of philosophy, and on receiving an answer to the effect that he knows that rain is wet and fire burns, replies: 'Such a one is a natural philosopher' (3.2.28; meaning simultaneously an original, untaught, and foolish philosopher. Word-plays where 'natural' means foolish occur in Act 1, scene 2 of the same comedy [ll. 41-46]). Touchstone then proves, through a chain of logical arguments, that the shepherd is damned because he has never been at court. Whether the poet's mockery, in keeping with Jacques' expression, flies aimlessly like a wild goose, 'unclaimed of any man', or whether he had particular philosophers in his sights, can hardly be established. It almost seems as though the 'natural philosopher' might allude to the great Francis Bacon, Lord Verulam. At that time, admittedly, only a few of the latter's *Essays* (1597) had appeared – Bacon's other writings were printed only after Shakespeare's death – but his main works had been completed much earlier (e.g. *The Advancement of Learning*, 1605) and his philosophical views must have been known in outline much earlier, perhaps so incompletely that when Shakespeare composed this comedy, probably in 1599, he could feel impelled to make this satirical attack, for after all Bacon's great authority as a philosopher emerged only much later, initially in foreign countries. It has certainly been claimed that a great spiritual kinship existed between Bacon and Shakespeare, to say nothing of the attempt to identify the two.[61] Yet, of the many parallel passages assembled from Shakespeare and Bacon's *Essays*, very few betray even a similarity, far less any sign of indebtedness. Even if some of Shakespeare's views agree with Bacon's, e.g. in advocating mutual help or in disliking extremes, there is nothing particularly distinctive in this, and the application of these principles to philosophy, setting up public utility as a standard,[62] is something Shakespeare seems not to have adopted; he seems rather to have assigned philosophy a more abstract value, as the utterances already quoted suggest. Perhaps Touchstone's discussion is intended to ridicule the ideal of philosophical utility.[63]

---

[61] W. H. Smith, *Was Lord Bacon the Author of Shakespeare's Plays?* (London, 1856); idem, *Bacon and Shakespeare* (London, 1857).
[62] Johann Eduard Erdmann, *Grundriss der Geschichte der Philosophie*, 2nd ed. (Berlin, 1869-1870), vol. 1, pp. 561, 562.
[63] Bacon's far from admirable moral character and his hostility to Essex, Southampton's friend and Shakespeare's patron,

Moreover, it was undoubtedly compatible with the poet's outlook that one cannot demand too much of philosophy and must accept that much remains inaccessible even to the most profound philosophical enquiry (cf. *Hamlet* 1.5.168, 2.2.350-351; *All's Well* 2.3.1-5).

Among contemporary philosophers, therefore, it was not Bacon, later the most famous of them, on whom Shakespeare relied; but a far greater influence than any of the philosophers known at that time was exerted on him by another contemporary, Giordano Bruno. This of course is to leave aside the general impact that Aristotelian philosophy retained in the literary world, without any need to assume a special study of the writings of its originator. To demonstrate this influence, something must first be said about Bruno himself, his writings and his teaching.

Giordano Bruno or Bruni was born in 1548 at Nola near Naples. He entered the Dominican Order

---

indicate that Shakespeare cannot have found him congenial, as a person or otherwise. Cf. Thomas Babington Macaulay, 'Lord Bacon' (1837), in *The Works of Lord Macaulay, Complete*, ed. Lady Trevelyan (New York, 1866), vol. 6, pp. 135-245 (on p. 168). Bacon himself never once mentions Shakespeare, who was only three years his junior, although he talks repeatedly about the theatre of his day. Given their social positions and their relations with Southampton, it can be assumed that they knew each other, perhaps personally: cf. Carl Karpf, *Το τί ήν είναι. Die Idee Shakespeare's und deren Verwirklichung. Sonetterklärung und Analyse des Dramas Hamlet (Indirecter Beitrag zur Zeitfrage 'Glauben und Wissenschaft')* (Hamburg, 1869), pp. 13-15.

at an early age, but thanks to his lively, indeed ardent imagination and his enthusiasm for nature and for Copernicus' discoveries he soon came into conflict with his spiritual superiors, from whom he first escaped by taking flight. He now led a nomadic life, publicizing his opinions at various places in France, Germany and Switzerland in academic and private lectures and in sundry writings. Towards the end of 1583 he arrived in London, armed with recommendations from King Henri III of France to the ambassador Mauvissière, was well received by the latter, and spent in his house the happiest and quietest period of his turbulent life. He remained there, apart from a few months spent in lectures and disputations in Oxford, till late in 1585, when the ambassador was summoned home. Bruno accompanied him to Paris, going later to Marburg and then to Wittenberg, where from August 1586 to April 1588 he delivered public lectures on philosophy, mathematics and physics. He often refers gratefully to the kindly and liberal welcome he received from the university teachers in Wittenberg, which he calls the German Athens, and this deserves particular emphasis, since the reference to Wittenberg in *Hamlet* should perhaps be traced back to Giordano Bruno.[64] In other places, Bruno was obliged to suffer persecution for his teaching;

---

[64] Cf. Tschischwitz, *Shakspere-Forschungen*, vol. 1: *Hamlet*, p. 53. Domenico Berti, *Vita di Giordano Bruno* (Florence, Turin, Milan, 1868), pp. 207ff.

he was driven out of Marburg at the behest of the professors there, and finally, in Venice, where a pupil, Mocenigo, had invited him, he was denounced by the latter, arrested in his house, and handed over to the Inquisition (1592). During seven years' imprisonment he withstood all its tortures and all its pressure to recant his teachings, and finally, having been delivered to Rome, he was burned alive, enduring it with the utmost courage and without uttering a cry of pain; on hearing his sentence pronounced, he uttered the memorable words to his judges: 'You show more fear by your sentence than I do on hearing it.'[65]

In Bruno's life, particular interest for our knowledge of Shakespeare and of conditions in England at that time attaches to his residence in London and what he relates about it. As is clear from his welcome in the ambassador's house and the favour he enjoyed from the latter, he came in contact

---

[65] Berti, *Giordano Bruno*, p. 263. [König's discussion here is rather swayed by the Italian Risorgimento image of a fearless Bruno, champion of liberty and free thought (on and around p. 263 Berti's picture is rather more nuanced). It does, however, tally with Berti's account of Bruno's death in his next chapter. Bruno's famous words: 'Maggior timore provate voi nel pronunciar la sentenza contro di me, che non io nel riceverla' (literally, 'You *feel* more fear ...') are reported by Berti on p. 293. Much more has been published on Bruno's life and trial since König's time, from Vincenzo Spampanato, *Vita di Giordano Bruno: con documenti editi e inediti*, 2 vols (Messina, 1921) and Luigi Firpo, *Il processo di Giordano Bruno* (Naples, 1949) to Ingrid D. Rowland, *Giordano Bruno: Philosopher/Heretic* (New York, 2008).]

with many of England's highly placed and famous people. He was even introduced to the Queen, and seems often to have visited the court with Mauvissière and also without him. In several passages of his writings he bestows enthusiastic praise on Elizabeth's royal virtues and intellectual attainments, calling her the great Amphitrite, Diana, the earthly goddess, a sun among the stars, to which he compares other English women and ladies, expressing great admiration likewise for them.[66] He is no less complimentary to the English lords and knights, praising their intellectual attainments and pleasant manners, and particularly singling out Leicester, Walsingham, and Sir Philip Sidney.[67] According to his meticulous biographer, Berti, who, having access to Venetian archives and the records of the Inquisition's proceedings against him, was the first to describe Bruno's life with complete clarity, he was also acquainted with Edmund Spenser and Gabriel Harvey, but Berti also states explicitly that it is uncertain whether he knew Bacon and

---

[66] Cf. the sonnet after the dedication to the *Eroici furori*, in Bruno, *Opere*, ed. by A. Wagner, vol. 2, p. 312 [Gentile-Aquilecchia vol. 2, p. 951]; vol. 1, p. 144 [*La cena delle Ceneri*, Dialogue 2, Gentile-Aquilecchia vol. 1, pp. 67-69, however, Aquilecchia's note on this passage should be either disregarded or read in conjunction with Hilary Gatti's 'A Note on the Text', in her edition of *The Ash Wednesday Supper* (Toronto, 2018), pp. lvii-lxi] and p. 230 [*De la causa, principio e uno*, end of Dialogue 1, Gentile-Aquilecchia vol. 1, pp. 222-223].

[67] *Opere*, vol. 1, p. 145 [*Cena*, Dialogue 2, Gentile-Aquilecchia vol. 1, pp. 69-70].

Shakespeare.[68] We could have assumed the latter but for the fact that Bruno's residence in London fell before and during Shakespeare's first period of activity and probably before his acquaintance with Southampton, who was only twelve at the time of Bruno's departure.

Bruno treats unfavourably the professional scholars, especially the professors at Oxford, and the lower orders. He describes the former as pedants with boorish manners.[69] The brutality of the common people fills him with mild horror. At the opening of the *Cena delle Ceneri* he tells of walking through London and describes amusingly various disagreeable encounters with people in the streets, boatmen, and the like, as well as the defective state of the streets, the filth, and so forth. Interesting in this context is the name of his companion, Florio, who is obviously the same Italian language teacher and translator of Montaigne whom Shakespeare is said to have depicted as Holofernes in *Love's Labour's Lost*. The latter claim is made, at any rate, by some of the earlier commentators – Warburton, Farmer, and Steevens – and Nathan Drake concurs with them.[70] Malone, who held the contrary opinion, pointed out that Florio was a protégé of

---

[68] Berti, *Giordano Bruno*, p. 192.
[69] *Opere*, vol. 1, p. 179 [*Cena*, Dialogue 4, Gentile-Aquilecchia vol. 1, pp. 133-134].
[70] Nathan Drake, *Shakespeare and His Times* (Paris, 1838), p. 217. *Shakespeare's Plays and Poems*, Variorum Edition (London, 1821), vol. 4, pp. 479ff.

Southampton, so that Shakespeare would not have ventured to treat him with such ridicule. We cannot regard this reason as conclusive, although Malone's chronology, dating the play to 1594, makes it seem more appropriate than the probably correct view that locates the play in the early years of Shakespeare's theatrical activity in London. To support the identification of Holofernes with Florio, particular weight is placed on the latter's attacks on dramatic poets, especially in a preface where he is avenging some mockery he had suffered; here mention was made of a sonnet which, it has been suggested, may allude to Holofernes' poem (*Love's Labour's Lost* 4.2.53-58). Such an interpretation is far from certain; at any rate, it does not look as if the poet wished to provide a complete and easily recognizable portrait of the Italian, otherwise he would doubtless have included among the many scraps of foreign languages that Holofernes utters more from Florio's mother tongue than the little rhyme in praise of Venice which, to be sure (according to Delius's edition of Shakespeare), is taken from a book by Florio. Considering how rarely Shakespeare's mockery can be related to particular individuals, it would be an important discovery if Bruno's reference to Florio could serve to elucidate this question. But this is the case only to a small extent. As Bruno relates, Florio first spends a long time searching for him then waits for him, with another person, outside his lodging in order to take him to the dinner (which supplies the title *Cena delle Ceneri*, or *Ash Wednesday Supper*) at the house of 'Folco Grivello' (Fulke Greville).[71] As they sail along the Thames, Florio strikes up a love-song (*Dove senza me, dolce mia vita?* – Where without me, my sweet life) 'as if remembering former loves'.[72] When they finally arrive at their destination, having been delayed by the filthy streets and by taking the wrong route, they find the other guests already at table, and a pleasant jest is related concerning one of the three new arrivals.[73] This person is directed to the still unoccupied lowest seat at the table, but mistakes it for the highest and, out of modesty, insists that he would rather sit at the opposite end, i.e. at what is in fact the highest seat of all. Although Florio is not named here, it is clear that he is the protagonist in this story, for immediately afterwards we are told that he is sitting opposite the Knight who was in the highest seat, with the narrator, Teofilo, on his left – obviously the 'maestro Guin' who made a third on the dangerous

---

[71] [There had been a misunderstanding whereby Bruno, it seems, had been expecting them to pick him up for a midday meal, given up waiting for them, and gone to see other friends. He returned after dark and found them waiting for him to take him to supper (cf. *Cena*, Dialogue 2, Gentile-Aquilecchia vol. 1, pp. 52-53). The theme of *errors* in more than one sense is quite prominent in this passage of *The Ash Wednesday Supper*.]

[72] *Opere*, vol. 1, pp. 138, 139 [*Cena*, Dialogue 2, Gentile-Aquilecchia vol. 1, pp. 55-56].

[73] *Opere*, vol. 1, p. 150 [*Cena*, Dialogue 2, Gentile-Aquilecchia vol. 1, p. 82].

walk through London.[74] Florio does not appear in the further course of the narrative, unless he is concealed behind the mask of Bruno's pedant, but this is ruled out by the love-song ascribed to Florio, since the pedant is described as a misogynist. Though we cannot gather much from this reference to Florio, it would at least confirm that the Italian language teacher was a figure of fun, and would reveal also the conceited modesty which is a principal trait in the amusing figure of Holofernes, whose connection to Bruno will be explored further below. In his narrative, Bruno dwells with great disgust on the custom of heavy drinking and on the accompanying practices, which he finds ridiculous and distasteful (e.g. taking it in turns to drink from the same goblet).[75] In another text, too, Bruno attacks the excessive drinking and its customs in Germany, concluding: 'videbitur porcus porcorum in gloriam Ciacchi' [with reference to the Dantean

---

[74] [König here appears to be identifying Teofilo with 'Maestro Guin', though the latter is undoubtedly based on Oxford scholar Matthew Gwynne. Teofilo is generally taken (including by König – see next note) to be simply Bruno's spokesman, though he presents himself as a separate person from 'Il Nolano'.]

[75] *Ibid.* [It is Teofilo who describes this repugnant custom, professing himself much relieved that it was not followed at this supper.]

glutton].[76] Does it not seem as though such invective prompted the lines in *Hamlet* (1.4.16-18.4):

> And to my mind ... it is a custom
> More honoured in the breach than the observance.
> This heavy-headed revel east and west
> Makes us traduced and taxed of other nations.
> They clepe us drunkards, and with swinish phrase
> Soil our addition.

The majority of Bruno's writings date from the period of his residence in London, including the three most important that chiefly expound his philosophical doctrine: *La cena delle Ceneri*, whose narrative framework we have just mentioned, *De la causa, principio e uno*, and *De l'infinito, universo e mondi*. All three are cast in dialogue form and dedicated to the Ambassador Mauvissière. Also published in that period were *Lo spaccio della bestia trionfante* and *La cabala del cavallo Pegaseo*, both of which have more to do with satire than philosophy and are accordingly listed by Hallam under the literature of entertainment.[77] Finally there was the *Eroici furori*, a work in which philosophy and poetry are curiously mingled. The *Spaccio* and the *Eroici furori* are dedicated to Philip Sidney. Although the title-pages of all six works say they

---

[76] In the *Spaccio della bestia trionfante*, *Opere*, vol. 2, p. 247 [Dialogue 3 (in the last few pages of the *Spaccio*), Gentile-Aquilecchia vol. 2, p. 821].

[77] Henry Hallam, *Introduction to the Literature of Europe in the Fifteenth, Sixteenth, and Seventeenth Centuries* (Paris, 1839), vol. 2, p. 249.

were printed in Paris or Venice, their content and dates make it clear that they were composed in London and probably also printed and disseminated there. How far this was the case, can hardly be determined now, but at all events they were known to Shakespeare, as will be shown below. The fact that all six works were written in Italian reveals how widely known this language was at that time among England's nobility and educated class, for which these writings were obviously intended in the first instance. Bruno's other philosophical writings are composed in Latin. Individual editions of all his works have always been very rare; only in 1830 did the collection of his Italian writings, cited here, appear in two volumes edited by A. Wagner, and it is already out of print. The Latin writings have never been collected.[78] Nor was any reliable, coherent information available about Bruno's life, until Berti explored the Inquisition's records of Bruno's trials in Venice and published his book *Vita di Giordano Bruno* in 1868. This also explains why the older commentators on Shakespeare say nothing about

---

[78] The collection begun by Gfrörer (Stuttgart, London and Paris, 1834) came to a halt without including the most important writings. Erdmann, *Geschichte der Philosophie*, vol. 1, p. 544. [We now know that Bruno's works were rather less rare than it was previously thought: see Rita Sturlese, *Bibliografia, censimento e storia delle antiche stampe di Giordano Bruno* (Florence, 1987). Since König's time there has also been an exponential increase in editions of Bruno's works. For his output in Latin see Bruno, *Opere latine*, ed. Carlo Monti (Turin, 1980).]

any connection with Giordano Bruno and his writings.

Before we try to examine these connections in more detail, let us draw attention to some principal points of Bruno's teaching, which we find Shakespeare taking note of.

Bruno's philosophical system is principally based on that put forward by some ancient philosophers of the Eleatic school and later developed by Spinoza and Leibniz, to the effect that the whole world and all the bodies in it consist of atoms which enter into various combinations while themselves remaining unchanged. Hence all phenomena in the world, human beings, animals, things, are determined by the manner in which the atoms are combined, and no change ever occurs in the composition of any body, nor does any component cease to exist: there is only a change in the manner of their combination. There is no change in existence, only in the manner of existence. This applies equally to physical and to purely mental existence, and so the various qualities of body and mind, the diverse individualities of humanity, are produced only by the diverse, infinitely multifarious connections within matter that is infinitely divisible, and which changes only in its combinations, not in its substance. Thus it is said of one of the auditors in the fifth dialogue of *De la causa, principio et uno*: 'Whoever takes Poliinnio as Poliinnio lays hands not on a specific substance, but on a substance with specific relations and differences, so that this person, in number and quantity, composes a species.'[79]

In Shakespeare we find Bruno's atomism compressed in the words of the Duke to Claudio in *Measure for Measure* (3.1.19-21), whom he is consoling in prison:

> Thou art not thyself,
> For thou exist'st on many a thousand grains
> That issue out of dust.

Most of the German versions known to us assume that 'grains' is meant in the sense of vegetable matter.[80] This implies a fairly banal meaning which by no means justifies the preceding sentence 'Thou art not thyself'. Delius's explanation, 'You have no definite, intrinsic essence of your own, but depend on a thousand tiny things', obviously fails to satisfy. If, however, we understand the sentence in relation to Bruno's atomism, it makes good sense and fits its context, for this doctrine leads logically to the statement that man has no definite individuality, no singular self, but is only an accidental and short-lived conglomerate of alien particles. The only obstacles to our interpretation are grammatical and linguistic ones which, however, apply in some measure also to the conventional

---

[79] *Opere*, vol. 1, p. 288 [*Della causa*, Dialogue 5, Gentile-Aquilecchia vol.1, p. 334].

[80] [We have omitted the discussion of the German translations found at this point (p. 109) in König's *Jahrbuch* 11 essay. For Delius, see note 2 in chapter 1 above.]

explanation – namely, that 'on' does not usually mean 'through', by' or 'from', as most translators assume, although the expression 'to feed on' is used in a sense compatible with the customary translation. But, as Delius testifies in his Shakespeare Lexicon, 'on' is often used by Shakespeare for 'of', and vice versa, and it occurs in the very same sense as here in a passage from *The Tempest* (4.1.156-157):

> We are such stuff
> As dreams are made on,

where the meaning is perfectly clear and closely related to that in the passage under discussion. Whether 'exist' can be used in the sense of 'consist of' may be open to argument, but even if the sentence is interpreted as 'you live through, you exist by virtue of, the thousand atoms of which you are composed', it can still be related to atomism. Shakespeare's use of 'grain' in the sense of 'smallest part, atom', is attested by A. Schmidt in his Shakespeare Lexicon and clearly confirmed by the passages he quotes. Besides, the word 'atomies'/'atomi' occurs several times in Shakespeare with the meaning familiar to us: i.e., respectively, in *As You Like It* 3.2.211 and 3.5.13; and *Romeo and Juliet* 1.4.58.[81]

---

[81] [The spellings quoted are as per the Norton Shakespeare. *As You Like It* was first published in the 1623 First Folio, where the word appears as 'Atomies' (Comedies, p. 196) and

The basic features of Bruno's atomism are, moreover, distinctly and specifically alluded to in the following passages from *Hamlet*, to which Tschischwitz has already drawn attention. In the graveyard scene (at 5.1.187-195) Hamlet says: 'Why may not imagination trace the noble dust of Alexander till a find it stopping a bung-hole?' In response to Horatio's objection, ''Twere to consider too curiously to consider so', Hamlet continues: 'No, faith, not a jot; but to follow him thither with modesty enough, and likelihood to lead it, as thus: Alexander died, Alexander was buried, Alexander returneth into dust, the dust is earth, of earth we make loam, and why of that loam whereto he was converted might they not stop a beer-barrel?'[82]

This transmigration of matter is treated similarly by Hamlet in Act 4 (3.21-31), when he replies to the King's question about Polonius that the worms are eating his corpse. 'Your worm', he continues, 'is your only emperor for diet. We fat all creatures else to fat us, and we fat ourselves for maggots ... A man may fish with the worm that hath

---

'atomyes' (p. 199). *Romeo and Juliet*'s 'atomi' (part of Mercutio's famous 'Queen Mab' speech) is attested in the early quartos of 1597 and (in mangled form) 1599 in ways that have extremely interesting implications. On this, see Elisabetta Tarantino's forthcoming chapter in a volume on Shakespeare and Italy edited by John Cameron.]

[82] On Alexander, it may be remarked that his dissolution into atoms is also a topic of Marcus Aurelius' meditations. Cf. Moriz Carrière, *Die Kunst im Zusammenhang der Kulturentwicklung*, vol. 2, p. 603.

eat of a king, and eat of the fish that hath fed of that worm.' Asked what he means by this, he answers: 'Nothing but to show you how a king may go a progress through the guts of a beggar.'

Bruno pursues the idea of the transmigration of matter with similar minuteness in a passage of his *Della causa, principio e uno*: 'Do you not see that what was seed becomes grass, what was grass becomes corn, what was corn becomes bread, what was bread becomes chyle, what was chyle becomes blood? that from this comes seed, thence the embryo, thence the human being, thence again the corpse, thence the earth, which becomes stone or some other thing, and that in this way they assume every natural form?'[83] Holding this view, Bruno could grant the body no cessation of existence, no death, but only a changed existence, of which he speaks distinctly in the following passage from the *Cena delle Ceneri*, thus helping further to gloss Hamlet's observations:

> Since the entire matter that composes our globe is capable neither of death nor of dissolution, and the annihilation of the whole of nature is impossible, it happens from time to time that that matter is renewed according to a definite order, changing, altering and rearranging all its parts, which must happen in a definite sequence whereby each thing takes the place of all others.[84]

---

[83] [*Della causa*, Dialogue 3, Gentile-Aquilecchia vol. 1, p. 267.]
[84] [*Cena*, Dialogue 5, Gentile-Aquilecchia vol. 1, p. 155.]

This explanation receives additional clarity from Bruno's principle that the world and nature are everywhere and at all times in motion.

These reflections, which the poet shows Hamlet to have absorbed, may be connected with the fact that Hamlet has studied in Wittenberg, where Bruno was once active for a longer period than elsewhere. They help to explain the indifference that Hamlet displays, not only towards the deaths of others (Polonius, Guildenstern), but also in thinking of his own. His words on the latter subject – 'If it be now, 'tis not to come. If it be not to come, it will be now. If it be not now, yet it will come. The readiness is all. Since no man has aught of what he leaves, what is't to leave betimes?' (5.2.158-161) – show similarities to the following words by Bruno (which are in themselves reminiscent of Shakespeare) from the dedication to *Candelaio*: 'This philosophy elevates my mind and extends my intellect. Therefore, whatever may be the time of the evening that I am awaiting, if the mutation is true, being in night I look forward to day, and those in daylight look forward to night. Everything that is, is either here or there, near or far, now or later, soon or afterwards.'[85]

---

[85] *Opere*, vol. 1, p. 5. [Con questa filosofia l'animo mi s'aggrandisce, e mi si magnifica l'intelletto. Però, qualunque sii il punto di questa sera che aspetto, se la mutazione è vera, io che son ne la notte aspetto il giorno, e quei che son nel giorno aspettano la notte. Tutto quel ch'è o è qua o là, o vicino o lungi, o adesso o poi, o presto o tardi.]

When one considers Hamlet's above-quoted utterances, one may easily feel that these, and Bruno's entire doctrine, are by no means compatible with Hamlet's famous monologue 'To be, or not to be', or with the appearance of the Ghost. On this point, we do not share Tschischwitz's assumption that Hamlet in his monologue rejects an indifferent attitude to death; rather, we think that such indifference supervenes towards the end of the play, together with a certain apathy in Hamlet's whole demeanour, while in the first three Acts Hamlet is often afflicted by fits of passion. On the other hand, we may find an explanation by supposing that the monologue, as we noted in a previous *Jahrbuch* essay (vol. 6, p. 297), stems from an earlier period and was retained for its theatrical effect. In introducing the Ghost, Shakespeare was following quite different notions from the sphere of popular belief, being guided by purely dramatic considerations without feeling obliged to reconcile this motif with Hamlet's philosophical reflections.

In general, it is not remotely likely that Shakespeare wished to shape his poetic creations, or even individual characters, entirely in conformity with Giordano Bruno's philosophical system. His knowledge of human nature was too extensive for that, and his main concern was with dramatic effect.

It might fairly be objected that our present discussion has no significant implications, for the evidence that Shakespeare knew Giordano Bruno and occasionally placed his doctrines in the mouths of various characters does not help us in the least to understand Shakespeare's mind; at most it furnishes further evidence for the poet's high level of education, something that used so often to be questioned. Yet Bruno's doctrine clearly influenced the poet's outlook and manner of expression, especially in the area where Shakespeare shows his greatest strength, that of character and its development. In this realm we find both men in such agreement on profound psychological phenomena that it seems unquestionably interesting to pursue Bruno's remarks on perceptions that Shakespeare mentions and touches on more or less clearly without explaining them in detail, something that he had no occasion to do as a poet.

First, Bruno's above-mentioned view, which he formulates clearly with respect to mental entities, emerges clearly from various passages in Shakespeare, especially in *Hamlet* and in plays belonging to the same period. Antony, standing beside Brutus' body, says: 'the elements *[were]* | So mixed in him that nature might stand up | And say to all the world "This was a man"' (*Julius Caesar*, ending – 5.5.72-74). Similarly Hamlet, speaking of Horatio's character: 'blest are those | Whose blood and judgement are so well commingled' (*Hamlet* 3.2.61-62), etc. Reproaching himself for his own shortcomings, Hamlet explains them by his deficient composition: 'I ... lack gall | To make oppression bitter' (2.2.554-555), but in this passage, alongside Bruno's teaching, we detect the view, common at that time, that certain passions and psychological forces had their seat in specific bodily organs. Comparing the two kings (3.4.59), Hamlet speaks of '[a] combination and a form' and, when he wishes for death, of 'this too too solid flesh' melting and resolving itself 'into a dew' (1.2.129-130), that is, not of perishing, but of entering into another combination, albeit one close to the dissolution of a solid body and the complete disappearance that he desires.[86] Edmund in *Lear* (1.2.12) expresses his satisfaction with his own way of being by saying that he was endowed with 'More composition and fierce quality' than legitimate sons, and the King in *All's Well That Ends Well*, wishing to praise Bertram's appearance, says (1.2.20-21):

> Frank nature, rather curious than in haste,
> Hath well composed thee.

When Lady Macbeth wishes for the ability to resolve on and carry out murder at *Macbeth* 1.5.35-52, her words imply the same outlook. See especially:

> Come to my woman's breasts,
> And take my milk for gall, you murd'ring ministers,
> Wherever in your sightless substances

---

[86] The King in *Hamlet* also regards death only as a change of form (1.2.72-73): 'Thou know'st 'tis common – all that lives must die, | Passing through nature to eternity.'

> You wait on nature's mischief.
> (*Macbeth* 1.5.45-48)

Finally, we find many formulations in the Sonnets which seem to imagine individuality, whether physical or mental, as based on a compound, e.g.:

> Sonnet 45: life's composition
> Sonnet 53: What is your substance, whereof are you made
> Sonnet 59: this composèd wonder of your frame
> Sonnet 71: When I perhaps compounded am with clay
> Sonnet 81: Although in me each part will be forgotten
> Sonnet 89: To set a form upon desirèd change

Bruno's atomism readily implies the claim, which he also made explicitly, that whatever exists has existed for ever, that nothing entirely disappears but only changes its location and its combinations as it makes room for other bodies, and that nothing whatever persists in the same condition. We find this in the following passages from the Sonnets, as well as in others, some of which will be discussed below:

> Sonnet 59: If there be nothing new
> Sonnet 60: Each changing place with that which goes before | In sequent toil all forwards do contend.

In this somewhat mechanistic view of the formation of character, Shakespeare ascribes faulty qualities especially to a predominance of individual elements, an exaggeration of qualities which are harmless in themselves, as in *Hamlet* 1.4.18.11: 'o'ergrowth of some complexion'. Here and in many other passages it is more or less clearly stated that such a fault, so to speak, infects and corrupts the other qualities, including virtues. This is especially apparent whenever Shakespeare portrays characters. When he wishes to portray ideals, he endows his favourites with a harmonious balance among their qualities, with moderation and restraint, as with Henry V, Portia, and others. The corresponding deficiencies in Shakespeare's characters reveal the same principle, indeed to an even greater extent, since the poet was too convinced of the imperfection of human nature to acknowledge any perfectly ideal characters.

The recurrent opinions in Shakespeare's works which we must necessarily relate to the poet's personality include the distinctive ambivalence, the truly philosophical endeavour to regard everything in two aspects, recognizing evil in good and good in evil. Here he reveals a particular intellectual affinity with Bruno, though, in keeping with their different vocations, it takes different forms in either of them. While Bruno, in a somewhat sophistical manner, often tries to demonstrate that something has a character contrary to its appearance, Shakespeare tends to remain within the limits of experience, though in dealing with this theme he can be somewhat obscure. As Bruno points out that a curved line at its utmost extension is closest to a straight line, Shakespeare shows, sometimes in casual references, sometimes in prominent and lengthy reflections, that when moral and intellectual qualities are taken to extremes, they are transformed into their opposite. Bruno discusses this ambivalence in a long disquisition in [Dialogue 5 of] *Della causa, principio e uno* (*Opere*, vol. 1, pp. 286ff.), which we reproduce here (partly *verbatim*, partly in an abridged version) so as to reveal Shakespeare's belief and its relation to Bruno's teaching:

> The intellect, man's power of discernment, in trying to free itself from the imagination, seeks to derive the multiplicity of phenomena from a common root. Thus Pythagoras traced everything back to numbers, Plato to the geometrical point. The former method is preferable because it can be applied also to the point and to all phenomena whatsoever [cf. Gentile-Aquilecchia vol. 1, pp. 330-331].

> In investigating any matter it is the business of the intellect to simplify it as much as possible, to abstract from its composition and quantity, and to consider not so much its accidental and changeable qualities, its dimensions and external relations, but rather that on which they are based [p. 332].

> When we aspire and strive towards the principle and the true substance of things, we make progress towards indivisibility. We will only attain to the primal matter and the universal substance when we arrive at the single indivisible substance in which everything is contained [p. 333].

> Substance and being are separate from quantity; measure and number are not themselves substance, but only relate to substance; they are not existent things, but grounds of existence. Thus substance is essentially without number or measure, and hence it is one and the

> same in all particular things that derive their individuality from number, as from something that lies outside substance. Hence a specific person is not a particular substance,[87] but substance in a particular relation, and it is through differences that lie outside substance, by virtue of number and quantity, that he is assigned to a specific species. Certain external events cause different kinds of substance to multiply [pp. 334-335].
>
> Yet at bottom it is one and the same in all things, just as every number can be traced back to the unity which, on being repeated, with limited things produces a number, with unlimited things negates number [p. 335].

Bruno now demonstrates with reference to various geometrical figures that in the largest and smallest things the opposites disappear, and continues:

> The principle of heat is something indivisible and hence different from all individual heat, because the principle is something other than the object to which it is applied. If that is so, who can hesitate to affirm that the principle is neither cold nor hot, but the same thing as cold and heat? Whence is it that one contrary is the principle of the other, and that therefore changes proceed in a cyclical manner, but from the fact that each is a subject, a principle, an end, a continuation and a conjunction of the other? The least degree of heat and the least degree of cold are one and the same; once the end or goal of the greatest heat has been reached, the movement towards cold begins. Hence it is clear, not only that the two utmost degrees meet each other in opposition and

---

[87] [The actual text here refers to 'Poliinnio' rather than a generic 'person', in a sentence that has been quoted previously.]

the two least degrees meet each other in agreement, but also that the greatest and the least meet each other in the vicissitude of transformation; wherefore physicians, encountering the healthiest body, have reason to be anxious, and prudent people are most anxious when they attain the highest degree of happiness. Who does not see that the principle of corruption and that of generation are one and the same? Is not the end of corrupt matter the beginning of created matter? Do we not say at the same time: one thing is taken, another is fetched; one thing was, another is? Certainly, if we apply the right measure, we will see that corruption is nothing but generation, and generation nothing but corruption: love is a form of hatred, and hatred is ultimately a form of love. To love something that one finds congenial means to hate its contrary; love of the latter is hatred of the former. In essence and origin, then, love and hatred, friendship and strife, are one and the same thing. Where does the physician seek the best antidote, but in the poison itself? Whence do we obtain the best theriac, but from the viper? The strongest poisons contain the best remedies. Does not one force come from two mutually opposed objects? Why should this be, but because the principle of existence is one and the same, just as the principle whereby either object is conceived of is one and the same, and that contraries relate to one subject in the same way that they are apprehended by one and the same perception? And I will not launch into a demonstration of how the spherical form depends upon the plane surface, the hollow on the convex, that the angry man is one with the patient man, the proudest man is most congenial to the modest man, and the miser to the generous man.

The result is that whoever wishes to investigate nature's greatest mysteries must seek and contemplate them in the contraries presented by the greatest and smallest things! A deep magic lies in the presentation of contraries after one has first found the point at which they are united [pp. 338-340].[88]

When we read this disquisition by Bruno, must it not seem as though Shakespeare's Friar Laurence were conceived as a devotee of his philosophy, perhaps even as the itinerant philosopher himself in a monk's garb, when the following words are placed in his mouth (*Romeo and Juliet* 2.2.8-26):

> ... baleful weeds and precious-juicèd flowers.
> The earth, that's nature's mother, is her tomb.
> What is her burying grave, that is her womb,
> And from her womb children of divers kind
> We sucking on her natural bosom find,
> Many for many virtues excellent,
> None but for some, and yet all different.
> O mickle is the powerful grace that lies
> In plants, herbs, stones, and their true qualities,
> For naught so vile that on the earth doth live
> But to the earth some special good doth give;
> Nor aught so good but, strained from that fair use,
> Revolts from true birth, stumbling on abuse.
> Virtue itself turns vice being misapplied,
> And vice sometime's by action dignified.
> Within the infant rind of this weak flower
> Poison hath residence, and medicine power,
> For this, being smelt, with that part cheers each part;
> Being tasted, slays all senses with the heart.

---

[88] Bruno speaks similarly in the *Spaccio della bestia trionfante*, Dialogue 1, *Opere*, vol. 2, p. 132 [cf. Momus' speech, in Gentile-Aquilecchia vol. 2, pp. 594-595].

Romeo himself seems also to have taken lessons from Bruno, when we consider how contraries are linked in this declamation (1.1.169-174):

> Why then, O brawling love, O loving hate,
> O anything of nothing first create;
> O heavy lightness, serious vanity,
> ...
> Still-waking sleep, that is not what it is!

From the numerous other passages in which Bruno's opinions are more or less clearly repeated, the following may be singled out:

> Before the curing of a strong disease,
> Even in the instant of repair and health,
> The fit is strongest. Evils that take leave,
> On their departure most of all show evil.
> (Pandolf in *King John* 3.4.112-115).

>   To be worst,
> The lowest and most dejected thing of fortune,
> Stands still in esperance, lives not in fear.
> The lamentable change is from the best;
> The worst returns to laughter.
> (Edgar in *King Lear* 4.1.2-6)

> Sweet are the uses of adversity,
> Which, like the toad, ugly and venomous,
> Wears yet a precious jewel in his head.
> (Duke Senior in *As You Like It* 2.1.12-14)

> There is some soul of goodness in things evil,
> Would men observingly distil it out –
> ...

Thus may we gather honey from the weed
And make a moral of the devil himself.
>   (King Harry in *Henry V* 4.1.4-12)

Most subject is the fattest soil to weeds.
>   (King Henry in *2 Henry IV* 4.3.54)

The strawberry grows underneath the nettle.
>   (Ely in *Henry V* 1.1.61)

As surfeit is the father of much fast,
So every scope, by the immoderate use,
Turns to restraint.
>   (Claudio in *Measure for Measure* 1.2.106-108)

                We may outrun
By violent swiftness that which we run at,
And lose by over-running. Know you not
The fire that mounts the liquor till 't run o'er
In seeming to augment it wastes it?
>   (Norfolk in *Henry VIII* 1.1.141-145)

                The present pleasure,
By revolution low'ring, does become
The opposite of itself.
>   (Antony in *Antony and Cleopatra* 1.2.113-115)

Where joy most revels, grief doth most lament;
Grief joys, joy grieves, on slender accident.
>   (Player King in *Hamlet* 3.2.180-181)

And nothing is at a like goodness still,
For goodness, growing to a plurisy,
Dies in his own too much.
>   (King Claudius in *Hamlet* 4.7.95.3-95.5)

> The love of wicked friends converts to fear,
> That fear to hate.
> (Richard in *Richard II* 5.1.66-67)

> Sweet love, I see, changing his property,
> Turns to the sourest and most deadly hate.
> (Scrope in *Richard II* 3.2.131-132)

The passages just quoted, especially the last few, all deal with moral qualities and the formation of character. But a particularly interesting concurrence between Bruno and Shakespeare is found when they speak of a character suddenly being transformed from good to bad. It is well known that one of Shakespeare's special excellences, such as we can attribute to no other poet in the same degree, is that the characters he depicts can be observed and understood even as they change and develop. As a rule, such changes are gradual and inconspicuous, just as in life, and the instances in which a character and a person's disposition suddenly undergo a radical reversal are comparatively rare, even in Shakespeare and on the basis of tremendous events. As examples we can perhaps cite only Timon of Athens, and Angelo in *Measure for Measure*, along with the somewhat immature conception of Proteus in *The Two Gentlemen of Verona*. To a lesser extent, and developing in individual ways, transformations occur with Hamlet, Bertram in *All's Well That Ends Well*, likewise in Lear, Macbeth and Lady Macbeth, and then to a still slighter extent in the poet's other figures, till finally with the least significant figures there can be no question of any visible character development. We shall cite some particularly interesting passages, again recalling Bruno, which of course are best considered in relation to the theatrical presentation of such character changes (in other persons), for only then does it become wholly clear to what a profound understanding the poet gives expression. In *Henry VIII* the King speaks as follows about a fairly minor character, Buckingham, applying the sentiment to him incorrectly because of a misconception (1.2.112-119):

> The gentleman is learnèd, and a most rare speaker,
> To nature none more bound; his training such
> That he may furnish and instruct great teachers
> And never seek for aid out of himself. Yet see,
> When these so noble benefits shall prove
> Not well disposed, the mind growing once corrupt,
> They turn to vicious forms ten times more ugly
> Than ever they were fair.

Likewise, Sonnet 94 says:

> But if that flower with base infection meet
> The basest weed outbraves his dignity;
> For sweetest things turn sourest by their deeds.

Besides some passages that have already been quoted (*Romeo and Juliet* 2.2.8-26; *2 Henry IV* 4.3.54; *Richard II* 3.2.131-132), there are more where the poet describes gifts and qualities, good in themselves, as 'traitors' when they are applied to bad uses (*All's Well That Ends Well* 1.1.37-39; *As You Like It* 2.3.10-15).

We have pointed out elsewhere that these passages repeat the old axiom *corruptio optimi pessima*, and have elucidated them by quoting some passages from Dante (*Purgatorio* 30.109, 118-120; *Paradiso* 8.93, 159; *Inferno* 31.55) and Plato (*Republic*, Book 6).[89] The clearest and closest concurrence with what Shakespeare says about the subject in the above quotations is in Giordano Bruno's first dialogue in *Della causa, principio e uno* (*Opere*, vol. 1, p. 222). There Filoteo, having rebutted the charge of representing the English people insultingly (in the *Cena delle Ceneri*), points out that it is alongside the very best behaviour that the worst is found: in Italy, for example, where virtue, learning and good behaviour are nourished and nurtured by everyone, vice, deceit, avarice and cruelty have also flourished in the highest degree. Thereupon Elitropio confirms Filoteo's claim, though unfortunately without adding any further explanation:

> That is quite right according to the principles of your philosophy, by virtue of which the contraries meet in the principle and subjects close to each other, because the same minds that are best disposed for sublime, virtuous and noble deeds, when once they are corrupted, fall into the contrary, extreme vices. Besides, we

---

[89] See my *Shakespeare als Dichter*, pp. 229ff. The relevant passages are also cited in the *Jahrbuch* 7, pp. 174ff.

usually find the rarest and most excellent minds where the most ignorant and foolish are, and where people in general are less cultivated and behave worse, we meet some with the greatest refinement and cultivation, so that it appears as though the same measure of perfection and imperfection were bestowed in different ways on many generations.[90]

From the beliefs and statements by Bruno and Shakespeare that have been discussed so far, it follows automatically – as is indicated clearly enough in some of the passages quoted here, e.g. *Romeo and Juliet* 2.2.8ff – that nothing is good or evil in itself, and Shakespeare has given this idea lapidary expression in other well-known passages, e.g. *Hamlet* 2.2.244-245 or *The Merchant of Venice* 5.1.98. Bruno puts this just as clearly: taken absolutely, nothing is imperfect or evil – it appears so only in relation to something else, and what is evil for one person is good for another; also: nothing is so bad that it cannot serve the use and advantage of good people, and nothing so good and valuable that it could not provide evil people with cause and matter for offence. This says in prose the same as Shakespeare puts in poetic form in some of the passages quoted above (e.g. *Henry V* 4.1.4-12; *As You like It* 2.1.12-14). Since we are here talking of good as a relative concept, it deserves to be mentioned that Shakespeare does once speak of the thing in itself. Lear says to Edgar, who is dressed –

---

[90] [Gentile-Aquilecchia vol. 1, pp. 205-206.]

or rather, virtually naked – as a beggar: 'Ha! here's three on's are sophisticated! Thou art the thing itself; unaccommodated man is no more but such a poor, bare, forked animal as thou art' (*King Lear* 3.4.97-100).[91]

This mocking reference to 'the thing itself' is entirely in accord with the poet's habit of assigning things only relative value; clearly he intended here to poke fun at particular philosophical discussions or tendencies, but there is no further clue to help identify his target. Yet even here an antagonism towards Bacon's philosophy and an indebtedness to Bruno's teaching could be inferred.

Rich as Shakespeare is in *sententiae*, we can point to few genuinely philosophical statements in his works, and it goes without saying that such statements can only rarely find a place in dramatic dialogue. The few such statements offered in his works, however, often show a relation to Bruno's teaching. Here we should like first to draw attention to Hamlet's utterance: 'to know a man well were to know himself' (*Hamlet* 5.2.102.31-32). The sentence permits many interpretations and may prompt a variety of reflections. We propose the simplest explanation: that man has only in himself the measure by which to understand others, whether moral or intellectual qualities are in question. If he is richly endowed with such qualities, and their nature

---

[91] On the use of 'unaccommodated' here, see *Jahrbuch* 9, p. 213n [here chapter 1, note 26].

is honest and wise, he will judge others all the more fairly and honestly, and the practice of judging others will give him the opportunity to become familiar with the means of judging, with his own abilities and qualities, and will thus increase his self-knowledge. In this manner Shakespeare at other points sheds light on this statement, indicating particularly that self-knowledge is to be sought in various respects through the knowledge of others. In *Henry VIII* (2.2.21) Suffolk replies to Norfolk's observation that the King will get to know Wolsey with the words:

> Pray God he do. He'll never know himself else.

Ulysses in *Troilus and Cressida* (3.3.90-97) mentions the statement by an author, described as a 'strange fellow', whom he is reading, that a richly endowed person recognizes his gifts as his own only in the light of others' approval, to which Achilles replies:

> The beauty that is borne here in the face
> The bearer knows not, but commends itself
> To others' eyes. Nor doth the eye itself,
> That most pure spirit of sense, behold itself,
> Not going from itself; but eye to eye opposed
> Salutes each other with each other's form.
> For speculation turns not to itself
> Till it hath travelled and is mirrored there
> Where it may see itself.
>   (*Troilus and Cressida* 3.3.98-106)

Ulysses agrees, saying the statement is not new, only the conclusion drawn by the author that nobody is the master of anything until he has communicated it as a gift to others:

> Nor doth he of himself know them for aught
> Till he behold them formèd in th'applause
> Where they're extended – who, like an arch, reverb'rate
> The voice again; or, like a gate of steel
> Fronting the sun, receives and renders back
> His figure and his heat.
> (113-118)

Similar ideas and images pervade the dialogue between Brutus and Cassius (*Julius Caesar* 1.2.53-60), where Cassius makes Brutus aware of his abilities and of the task that they impose on him:

> CASSIUS ... Tell me, good Brutus, can you see your face?
> BRUTUS No, Cassius, for the eye sees not itself
> But by reflection, by some other things.
> CASSIUS 'Tis just;
> And it is very much lamented, Brutus,
> That you have no such mirrors as will turn
> Your hidden worthiness into your eye,
> That you might see your shadow.

It is true that this connection between self-knowledge and the knowledge of others has been treated by many philosophers, as well as by poets.[92]

---

[92] Goethe, speaking of Shakespeare, declares aptly: 'The highest goal that man can attain is the awareness of his own

Yet we think it important to state that Bruno, in the subtler expositions of his doctrine, arrives at the same conclusions as the reflections by Shakespeare quoted above. As we gather from the long disquisition quoted above from Bruno's *Della causa* (vol. 1, pp. 286ff), Bruno sees knowledge as consisting particularly in comparing and abstracting differences. Hence it follows that, since external phenomena are so numerous and diverse, reason can only arrive at accurate knowledge of the objective world by contemplating itself and thus gaining a unified and coherent representation, which it projects outwards. Thus the old saw *nosce te ipsum* is specially valuable, not only for one's own cultivation and capacity, but for the knowledge of other people and of humanity in general. Anyone who is not content with superficial perception of the external world, but wants to penetrate the inner essence of phenomena and comprehend their unity, must descend into the depths of his own inner being. Only there can he find the requisite general concepts, which in the external world lie scattered amid the medley of individual things and are

---

dispositions and ideas, the knowledge of himself, which first enables him to comprehend other people's temperaments.' ('Shakespeare und kein Ende', edition in 2 vols, vol. I, p. 610.) Antonio says in *Torquato Tasso* (2.3): 'No man can gain self-knowledge from within, | For, using his own measure, he will judge | Himself at times too small, or else too great. | Man knows himself only in other men; | Life only teaches each man who he is.'

perceptible only to him who already has them within himself.

Other individual opinions, which Shakespeare in his plays uses more superficially by assigning them to individual characters, and even then not always as their personal convictions, are clearly anticipated and explained in Bruno, and, though they sometimes occur among earlier philosophers, were probably taken by the poet from Bruno's writings. Thus the statement, mentioned by Bruno (vol. 2, p. 246), 'sol et homo generant hominem' was obviously in Shakespeare's mind when he made Hamlet warn Polonius not to let his daughter walk in the sun lest she conceive (2.2.185-186).[93] For the passionate invectives against women in *Hamlet* and elsewhere, too, it is obvious that Shakespeare is indebted to discussions by Bruno, especially in *Della causa*. There (*Opere*, vol. 1, p. 266) woman is connected or identified with matter and the man with form. Sin is traced back only to woman, i.e. matter, when Poliinnio says: 'Form does not sin and

---

[93] In an essay on this passage, T. Vatke points out that the sentence is of great antiquity and appears in Aristotle's *Physics* (2.2.14-15 194b): ἄνθρωπος γὰρ ἄνθρωπον γεννᾷ καὶ ἥλιος. Hence he thinks that Shakespeare's allusion rests on opinions widespread in his day concerning spontaneous generation and alchemy, and does not go back to Bruno. Although he quotes several illustrations from Ben Jonson, these refer only to spontaneous generation of animals; he produces no evidence that this statement was widespread, and Shakespeare is more likely to have taken it from Bruno than from Aristotle. Cf. Herrig, *Archiv für neuere Sprachen*, vol. 52, p. 39.

no form gives rise to a fault so long as it does not form a connection with matter.'[94] Accordingly, form, designated as male, says to *natura naturans* by way of exoneration [obviously echoing Adam in Genesis]: 'Mulier, quam dedisti mihi, i.e. the matter you gave me for company, ipsa me decepit, i.e. is the reason for all my sins.' Tschischwitz (*Shakspere-Forschungen*, vol. 1, p. 64) has already rightly related this passage and some similar ones to Hamlet's bitter invectives against Ophelia: 'Get thee to a nunnery … wise men know well enough what monsters you make of them' (*Hamlet* 3.1.122-139), besides the well-known 'frailty, thy name is woman' (1.2.146). Posthumus in *Cymbeline* (2.5.19-22) also ascribes all faults and sin to woman:

> Could I find out
> The woman's part in me – for there's no motion
> That tends to vice in man but I affirm
> It is the woman's part.

If, as we think we have sufficiently proved in the foregoing, Giordano Bruno as a philosopher in various ways influenced Shakespeare's formation and writing, the question arises whether Bruno's poetic works as such had any influence on Shakespeare, especially as both poets in the main cultivated the same genres of poetry. For Bruno's – admittedly not numerous – literary works consist of

---

[94] [*De la causa*, beginning of Dialogue 1, Gentile-Aquilecchia vol. 1, pp. 289-292 (on p. 291).]

sonnets and other short poems of similar form, and a comedy, *Il Candelaio* (The Candlemaker). The latter's poetic value, in relation to Shakespeare's plays, is indeed that of a single work compared to a large number. It was printed in 1582, in Paris according to the title-page, but was probably written earlier in Italy, as appears from its whole tone and from the local references it contains.[95] It seems to have found no particular favour with contemporaries, since we know of no performances and of only a few later adaptations. Nonetheless it can be assumed that, along with Bruno's philosophical writings, this work, in which, as Berti says, the philosopher Bruno is just as recognizable as the comic dramatist is in the philosophical writings, became well enough known in England to be available to Shakespeare, and that Shakespeare, since he got to know Bruno's other works, is all the more likely to have taken notice of his comedy.[96] There are also clear signs that the English poet knew the *Candelaio* and used some details from it in his own work. A parallel has already been drawn (p. 111 [in *Jahrbuch* 11]) between the dedication of the

---

[95] Berti, *Giordano Bruno*, p. 141.
[96] [For an update on Shakespeare and *Candelaio* see Hilary Gatti, 'Giordano Bruno's *Candelaio* and Possible Echoes in Shakespeare and Ben Jonson', *Viator* 43 (2012), 357-375; Elisabetta Tarantino, 'Shakespeare and Religious War: New Developments on the Italian Sources of *Twelfth Night*', *Shakespeare Survey* 72 (2019): 32-47; both with further references.]

Candelaio and some words uttered by *Hamlet*. Our attention is also caught by a dialogue in Act 2, scene 1 of the *Candelaio*, which finds a kind of echo in *Hamlet*. Octavio asks the pedant Manfurio: 'What is the matter (*materia*, meaning also 'content') of your verses?' to which the answer comes: 'litterae, syllabae, dictio et oratio, partes propinquae et remotae'; which then gives rise to the further question: 'I mean what is their subject and purpose?' In *Hamlet* (2.2.191-195) Polonius asks the Prince what he is reading and receives the answer 'Words, words, words', with further equivocation, whereupon Polonius says: 'I mean the matter you read, my lord.'[97] If such details, of small import in themselves, reinforce or extend the evidence for Shakespeare's acquaintance with Bruno's comedy, then, since it is indubitable that the Italian drama had considerable influence on the course of Shakespeare's formation as a playwright, we may include the *Candelaio* in this influence, though not as a major element. Although it is no masterpiece, indeed so flawed that Shakespeare could never have taken this play as a model, it is still not among the inferior productions of the Italian drama. It is dominated, hardly by a comic mood, but by a Mephistophelean irony and sarcastic humour, so that the author's epigraph seems entirely apt: 'in tristitia

---

[97] Similarly, with the same antithesis, in *Troilus and Cressida* (5.3.109-110): 'Words, words, mere words, no matter from the heart.'

hilaris, in hilaritate tristis', revealing, it would seem, the ambivalence to which we drew attention above. On the whole, Bruno's comedy has the same strengths and flaws as those of Pietro Aretino; it resembles his work in its weak characterization and its obscenities, but Bruno's manner is somewhat grander, approaching that of Ariosto.[98] The plot is confused and hard to follow, because it interweaves three different intrigues, recalling the sequence of scenes in some plays by Shakespeare, e.g. *The Merchant of Venice*. Among the figures in the comedy, the pedant stands out, and it is generally accepted that this figure, typical of the Italian comedy, was taken over by Shakespeare. Since the pedant is a common type, that would not in itself suggest a link with Bruno's comedy, but there are numerous similarities suggesting that Shakespeare based his pedant on Bruno's portrayal. Since Bruno, as may be gathered from what has already been said about him, had a very pronounced antipathy to all forms of pedantry, and particularly to learned pedantry – a trait which he shares with Shakespeare, as he does the accompanying profound devotion to truth and the hatred for all pretence and hypocrisy – he always introduces the figure of the pedant into his philosophical dialogues, attacking it with a diverse range of weapons and in every tone, from serious discussion to wit and satire. In the comedy the pedant is called Manfurio, in the dialogues

---

[98] Berti, *Giordano Bruno*, p. 153.

Poliinnio and Coribante, but at bottom they are one and the same person. The similarity of these names to Polonius and Corambis (the name Polonius bears in the first edition of *Hamlet*) has led Tschischwitz to connect Bruno's and Shakespeare's characterizations, and we are the more inclined to support this view because there are plenty of small features, also noted by him, which strengthen it. We have already mentioned the dialogue between Polonius and Hamlet [2.2.87-90], and it is noteworthy that the answer given by Bruno's pedant is assigned by Shakespeare to Hamlet, in order to ridicule the pedant. There is another feature of Polonius's speech that is probably traceable to Giordano Bruno, and which we have already discussed in the *Jahrbuch* (vol. 9, p. 211) [see chapter 1 above]. Bruno also provides a detailed description of the learned pedant, in which we recognize other traits and utterances of Polonius. When reading aloud the inscription to the love-letter sent by Hamlet to Ophelia, after dilating with particular self-satisfaction on Hamlet's emotional state, Polonius comments: 'that's an ill phrase, a vile phrase, "beautified" is a vile phrase' (*Hamlet* 2.2.111-112). Then, at suitable and unsuitable points during the player's declamation (2.2.478, 484, 499-500), he utters his judgement in the same manner, now approvingly, now disapprovingly, and sometimes, thanks to the contrast with the declamation, with a highly comical effect: e.g. 'This is too long', '"mobbled queen" is good'. Bruno's description of the pedant, to which we wish to relate the above-mentioned passages, is voiced by Filoteo in the first dialogue of *Della causa* (*Opere*, vol. 1, p. 227). The description being rather long, we shall give it in abbreviated form, but retaining the exact wording where the resemblance is most apparent. A further reason for such a lengthy quotation is that we shall presently relate it to yet another Shakespearean pedant. After briefly characterizing the other participants in the dialogue, Filoteo says of Poliinnio:

> This God-forsaken pedant is the fourth, one of the severest judges of philosophy, one to whom his herd of scholastics is greatly devoted, wherefore, from Socratic love, he calls himself the eternal foe of the female sex and thinks himself to resemble Orpheus, Musaeus, Tityrus and Amphion. He is one of those who, when they have constructed a good sentence, composed an elegant letter, or filched a fine phrase from Cicero's storehouse, would say of themselves: Democritus is risen from the dead, Tully is still flourishing, Sallust is living on; he is an Argus who takes note of every letter, every syllable, every turn of phrase; he is a Rhadamanthus who summons the shades of the dead – *umbras vocat ille silentum*; a Minos who *urnam movet*. Such people call speeches to be examined and discuss individual expressions with words such as: 'Only a poet can understand this, only a comedian that, this is for the orator! That is heavy, this is light, that is sublime, this is *humile dicendi genus*; this speech is rough, but it would be smooth if it were composed in this manner; that is a youthful writer who has studied antiquity but little, *non*

redolet Arpinatem, desipit Latium; this expression is not Tuscan, it does not come from Boccaccio, Petrarch or other models of writing. One writes not *homo* but *omo*, not *honore* but *onore*, not Polihimnio but Poliinnio.' So pleased are they with themselves that they like their own performances best; he is Jupiter, observing from his high seat the life of other people, which is subject to so many errors, misfortunes and needless labours; he alone is happy and leads a heavenly life, contemplating his divinity in the mirror of a lexicon or a literary anthology.[99] Endowed with such self-assurance, he sees every other person as a mere single being, but he is everything at once. When he laughs, he calls himself Democritus; when something grieves him, he is Heraclitus; when disputing, he calls himself Aristotle; when indulging his fantasy, Plato; when bleating a speech, Demosthenes; and when he construes Virgil, he himself is Maro. He corrects Achilles, approves of Aeneas, reprimands Hector, is angry with Pyrrhus, is sorry for Priam, discusses Turnus, excuses Dido, praises Achates, and when he replaces one word with another and arranges synonyms on a string, *nihil divinum a se alienum putat* and descends from the professorial chair like one who has ordered the heavens, ruled senates, mastered armies, and reformed worlds, and certainly it is only because of the injustice of the age that he does not indeed accomplish what he believes he is doing.[100]

Since Bruno provided such an amusing and elaborate portrait of the pedant, enhanced by vivid colouring in the comedy *Candelaio*, Shakespeare

---

[99] [Here Bruno names a number of works on grammar and rhetorics that were used in schools at the time. For details, see the note in Gentile-Aquilecchia vol. 1, p. 216.]

[100] [*Della causa*, Dialogue 1, Gentile-Aquilecchia vol. 1, pp. 215-217.]

must have been tempted to borrow some of its traits and colours for his own work. In particular, his Holofernes in *Love's Labour's Lost* has obviously received on his stiff back some lashes from the whip of the Italian philosopher. For, as the foregoing description indicates, he has much in common with Bruno's pedants, e.g. the severity with which he insists on correct orthography and pronunciation (5.1), and the inclusion in his speech of scraps of Latin, though with Manfurio they are even more plentiful. At times the curate Nathaniel assumes the role of the pedant, and in general he sings his schoolmaster's praises, commending an expression used by him much in the manner of Polonius: 'A most singular and choice epithet' (5.1.14). Another trait that has passed from Manfurio to Holofernes is this: Manfurio recites a very baroque poem on a slaughtered pig, improvising it as the original author, yet claiming to have imitated Ovid's description of the Calydonian boar. A counterpart to this production is Holofernes' alliterative poem on the deer shot by the Princess; he likewise claims with arrogant modesty to have extemporized it with ease, whereupon he comments on his own poetic talent and singles out Ovid as exemplary for elegance of diction and facility of versification (4.2.46-66; 112-117). Finally, it must not go unmentioned that in the work by Bruno the description of the pedant is closely followed by the injunction to him (*Opere*, vol. 1, p. 230) to abandon his misogyny as something absurd and contrary to nature, a motif that in *Love's Labour's Lost* is treated fully, especially in Biron's fine declamations (Acts 1 and 4).[101]

Although the similarities to which attention has been drawn convincingly indicate the influence Bruno exerted on the comic dramatist Shakespeare, alongside his philosophical influence on Shakespeare's entire intellectual development, the concurrence in individual instances could be coincidental, and life presents, and always has presented, so many pedants that Shakespeare might more conveniently have found his models for Holofernes, for example, in the classrooms of London or Stratford than in Italian comedies. Thus Florio, as set out above (pp. 104ff. [in *Jahrbuch* 11; see the discussion at the start of this chapter]), has been plausibly proposed as such a model, which of course by no means rules out the assumption that the poet was simultaneously following Bruno or other Italian comedies in giving this amusing portrayal of his pedant. In Bruno's comedy, however, we find another element that recurs in Shakespeare's work, and that Shakespeare could hardly have found anywhere else, certainly not in models from real life, though here, above all, such models seem in a

---

[101] [Towards the end of Dialogue 1 of *Della causa*,] Filoteo exclaims: Chi è più insensato e stupido, che quello che non vede la luce? Qual pazzia può esser più abietta, che per ragion di sesso esser nemico a l'istessa natura [come quel barbaro re di Sarza ...; Gentile-Aquilecchia vol. 1, p. 221.]

certain degree indispensable for even the most gifted poet. It is the fluent, lively, and extremely rapid speech and descriptive style of the ordinary man, of lower-class persons, which is peculiar to some of the Romance-speaking peoples, particularly to the Italians and, among them especially to the Neapolitans. In his comedy – especially when he gives speeches to persons of the lowest rank, and likewise to those of low morals who in the *dramatis personae* are listed as swindlers – and to some extent also in the dialogues, Bruno reproduces the everyday language of his native city to an extent that very few contemporary dramas can match. Shakespeare could find nothing similar among the lower classes of the English people, for neither then nor now is a similar manner of speaking to be found in the corresponding ranks of peoples of the Germanic race. Nonetheless, particularly in his early comedies, where the Italian influence still predominates, Shakespeare gives various lower-class persons this way of speaking and story-telling with the utmost naturalness, and a comparison of a few such passages shows, in our view, that Bruno served him as a model. In the *Candelaio* (Act 3, scene 8 [*Opere*, vol. 1, pp. 51–52, marked as scene 7]) Barra, one of the four swindlers who appear in the play, recounts a trick he played on a tavern owner, in the following manner:

> ... after eating, as I had no intention of paying, I said to the host, 'Host, I want to play a game!' 'What sort of

game shall we play?' said he, 'here are tarock cards.' I replied: 'I cannot win at this damned game because of my bad memory.' Said he: 'I also have ordinary cards.' I rejoined: 'They may be marked, so that you can recognize them; don't you have any that have not yet been used?' He answers: 'No. So let us think of another game. Listen, do you play draughts?' 'I know nothing about it.' 'Listen, do you play chess?' 'That game would make me deny Christ.' Then he flew into a passion. 'What kind of game do you want to play, devil take it? Suggest something.' Says I: 'Throwing the ball at the ring.' Said he: 'Why ball and ring? You can see there's no room here for such a game.' Said I: 'Morella?' 'That's a game for porters and swineherds.' 'With five dice?' 'Why the devil with five dice? I have never heard of such a game. If you want, we can play with three dice.' I told him that I never had any luck with three dice. 'In the name of fifty thousand devils!' said he, 'if you want to play, then suggest a game that we can both play.' I said to him: 'Let's play at splitting mussels.' 'Get away,' said he, 'you are making fun of me; that's a game for children, aren't you ashamed?' 'All right then,' said I, 'let's play at chasing each other.' 'You're still joking', said he, and I assured him by the blood of the Immaculate Virgin that that was what I wanted to play. 'If you are honest,' said he, 'pay me, and if you won't go with God, then go with the chief of all devils.' I said: 'By the holy blood, I want to play.' 'And I won't play', said he. 'And you must play', said I. 'And I will never, never play with you.' 'And you will play right here on this spot.' 'And I don't want to.' 'And you will want to.' And in the end, I began to pay him with my heels, *id est*, to run away.

... dopo che ebbi mangiato, non avendo troppo buona fantasia di pagare, dissi al tavernaio: Messer oste, vorrei giocare. A qual gioco, disse lui, volemo giocare? Qua ho de' tarocchi. Risposi: a questo maldetto gioco non posso vincere, per che ho una pessima memoria. Disse lui: ho di carte ordinarie. Risposi: saranno forse segnate, che voi le conoscerete. Avetene, che non siino state ancor adoperate? Lui rispose di no. Dunque pensiamo ad altro gioco. Ho le tavole, sai? Di queste non so nulla. Ho de' scacchi, sai? Questo gioco mi farebbe rinegar Cristo. Allora gli venne la senapa in testa. A qual dunque diavolo di gioco vorrai giocar tu? Proponi! Dico io: a stracquare a pallamaglio. Disse egli: come? a pallamaglio? vedi tu qua tali ordegni? Vedi luoco da posservi giocare? Dissi: a la morella. Questo è gioco da facchini, bifolchi e guardaporci. A cinque dadi. Che diavolo di cinque dadi? Mai udii di tal gioco. Se vuoi, giochiamo a tre dadi. Io gli dissi, che a tre dadi non posso aver sorte. Al nome di cinquantamila diavoli, disse lui, se vuoi giocare, proponi un gioco, che possiamo farlo e voi et io! Gli dissi, giocamo a spaccastrammola. Va, disse lui, che tu mi dai la baia: questo è gioco da putti; non ti vergogni? Orsù, dunque dissi, giocamo a correre. Or questa è falsa, disse lui; et io soggiunsi: al sangue de l'intemerata, che giocarai. Vuoi far bene? disse; pagami, e se non vuoi andar con dio, va col prior de' diavoli. Io dissi: al sangue delle scrofole, che giocarai. Eh che non gioco, diceva. Eh che giochi, dicevo. Eh che mai mai vi giocai. Eh che vi giocarai adesso. Eh, che non voglio. Eh che vorrai. In conclusione comincio io a pagarlo con le calcagne, id est a correre.

In *The Comedy of Errors* Dromio recounts his meeting with Antipholus (2.1.61-67) as follows:

> ''Tis dinner time', quoth I. 'My gold', quoth he.
> 'Your meat doth burn', quoth I. 'My gold', quoth he.
> 'Will you come home?' quoth I. 'My gold', quoth he;
> 'Where is the thousand marks I gave thee, villain?'
> 'The pig', quoth I, 'is burned.' 'My gold!' quoth he.

> 'My mistress, sir –' quoth I. 'Hang up thy mistress!
> I know thy mistress not. Out on thy mistress!'

Launce gives a similar recital in a monologue in *The Two Gentlemen of Verona* (4.4.17-19):

> 'Out with the dog', says one. 'What cur is that?' says another. 'Whip him out', says the third. 'Hang him up', says the Duke.

Launce adopts this lively manner of speaking in other passages when delivering soliloquies (2.3),[102] as does his spiritual kinsman Launcelot Gobbo in the monologue in *The Merchant of Venice* 2.2.1-25, which, like Bruno's Barra's, ends with 'running away' ('my heels are at your commandment'). In the later plays, however, such a manner of expression is scarcely to be found among the clowns, fools, and persons of low rank who provide the comic effects.

Hence it seems to us beyond doubt that Bruno also influenced Shakespeare in various ways as a comic dramatist. A closer investigation might demonstrate further examples, since in his philosophical writings Bruno also manages here and there to cast a clear light on comic traits that would

---

[102] [With reference to Poliinnio's mysoginistic speech from the beginning of Dialogue 4 of *De la causa* mentioned above and its pronouncement on sin pertaining to women as matter rather than men as form, it is worth adding that as part of this monologue Launce playfully ascribes the role of his mother to the shoe with a hole in it because 'it hath the worser *sole*' (*The Two Gentlemen of Verona* 2.3.15).]

repay study by any comic dramatist. For example, the portrayal of Doctor Nundinio opening the dispute in the *Cena delle Ceneri* ([at the start of] Dialogue 3, *Opere*, vol. 1, p. 151) is a delightful little genre sketch with relevance also for our age of societies, assemblies, and preparatory meetings with chairmen and secretaries: 'Now Doctor Nundinio, having struck a pose, wiggled his back a bit, gazed around, with both hands propped on the table, and moving his tongue somewhat in his mouth, raising his eyes in quiet serenity to the heavens, shaping his lips to a subtle smile, and having spat once, began as follows'.[103]

Finally, the present investigation must not entirely ignore Bruno's sonnets, even if they should contribute only a little to the interpretation of Shakespeare's, for, since our understanding of the latter is always in flux, anything that helps to strengthen it will be justified. Bruno's sonnets are scattered through his Italian works. Some are prefixed to his works as a kind of dedication or introduction, most are contained in the text *Degli eroici furori* and form its real content, inasmuch as the prose discussions are mainly intended to explain the poems. The entire work treats of the love of God in two sections, each of which is divided into five dialogues among different persons. The first part contains forty sonnets, the second a similar number of poems, some of which are likewise composed in

---

[103] [Gentile-Aquilecchia vol. 1, p. 85.]

sonnet form, others in various approximations to it. The poems are somewhat rough in their versification, and in places the metre is not followed exactly. The content of the work as a whole suffers from obscurity, and lacks the keenness of intellect that distinguishes Bruno's other works mentioned here, partly because of its mixture of forms. On the other hand, it conveys, especially in the sonnets, great enthusiasm and profound sensibility, and in the opinion of the best-qualified judges the sonnets contain a good deal of their author's inner life.[104] Similar claims, as is well known, have been made for Shakespeare's sonnets by some, but vehemently denied by others. Our view that part at least of Shakespeare's sonnets, including the richest and most interesting, are to be understood as expressing his own feelings, is reinforced by a comparison with Bruno's sonnets, and seems confirmed when we consider that if the sonnets were based on fictitious relationships, these would have to be indicated more clearly than is the case with Shakespeare and with similar poems by Italian authors. In Giordano Bruno and other Italians, such as Dante and Michelangelo, Shakespeare had models who made the sonnet into the expression of profound inward psychological and emotional states, while most of the English sonneteers earlier than or contemporary with Shakespeare treated only of conventional fictions

---

[104] Berti, *Giordano Bruno*, p. 187.

concerning love and friendship in their sonnets.[105] In this manner, if our view is accepted, he was probably influenced by Italian sonneteers. The affinities that have been shown here give us all the more reason to assume that Bruno also influenced him in this respect, and indeed individual sonnets by both poets are not only related in content but similar in some ideas and expressions. In Dialogue 2 of the First Part of the *Eroici furori*, where Bruno's poems describe the inner division of the soul that is not yet concentrated, the second sonnet (the tenth in the Dialogues overall) runs as follows:

> What a condition, destiny or state
> This living death and deathly life bestow!
> Love's struck me down (alas) with such a fate
> That neither death nor life is mine to know.
> Bereft of hope at Hell's infernal gate,
> And brimming with desire, to Heaven I go.
> Therefore, as contradiction's constant slave
> I'm exiled both from Heaven and the grave.
> My woes grant no reprieve
> Because at two wheels' whirling intersection,
> Each knocks me in the opposite direction.
> Ixion-like, I come and yet I leave:
> Ambiguous proceedings
> Where spur and rein inspire contrary readings.[106]

---

[105] See my *Shakespeare als Dichter*, p. 237, where I quote a specific sonnet by Michelangelo.

[106] [For this and the following sonnet we have borrowed Ingrid Rowland's inspired translation from her edition of *On the Heroic Frenzies* (Toronto, 2013), on pp. 71-73 and 91; the Italian is from Gentile-Aquilecchia vol. 2, pp. 979 and 993.]

> Ahi, qual condizion, natura, o sorte:
> In viva morte morta vita vivo!
> Amor m'ha morto (ahi lasso!) di tal morte,
> Che son di vita insieme e morte privo.
> Voto di spene, d'inferno a le porte,
> E colmo di desio al ciel arrivo:
> Talché suggetto a doi contrarii eterno,
> Bandito son dal ciel e da l'inferno.
> Non han mie pene triegua,
> Perché in mezzo di due scorrenti ruote,
> De quai qua l'una, là l'altra mi scuote,
> Qual Ixion convien mi fugga e siegua,
> Perché al dubbio discorso
> Dan lezïon contraria il sprone e 'l morso.

Here, as is said in other sonnets, most clearly in [Part I] Sonnet 7 of Dialogue 1, Love is imagined as the bestower of the purest happiness and the noblest goods, namely knowledge and truth. In the third dialogue [of Part I], which deals with the power of the will, which was previously divided but now turns decisively to the supra-sensual realm, the third sonnet (the fourteenth of the whole sequence) runs:[107]

> Alas! I'm forced by my insanity
> To cling to my delusion
> That makes Love seem the highest good to me.
> My soul in its confusion
> Persists in its conflicting inclinations.
> As for the cruel despot

---

[107] [It may simply be a coincidence, but the irregularity in the number of lines draws attention to the fact that with this sonnet we have reached a number of poems (if we disregard those in the paratext) that equals the number of lines in a regular sonnet.]

Who feeds me on starvation,
And bans me from myself without a respite:
His rule, not freedom, pleases.
I spread sail to the breezes
That sweep me far away from good I hate,
And toss me towards a sweet but deadly fate.

Oimè, che son constretto dal furore
D'appigliarmi al mio male,
Ch'apparir fammi un sommo ben Amore.
Lasso, a l'alma non cale,
Ch'a contrarii consigli unqua ritenti;
E del fero tiranno,
Che mi nodrisce in stenti,
E poté pormi da me stesso in bando,
Più che di libertade i' son contento.
Spiego le vele al vento,
Che mi suttraga a l'odioso bene,
E tempestoso al dolce danno amene.

Compare with this Shakespeare's Sonnets 129, 144, 148, 137, and especially 147:

My love is as a fever, longing still
For that which longer nurseth the disease,
Feeding on that which doth preserve the ill,
Th'uncertain sickly appetite to please.
My reason, the physician to my love,
Angry that his prescriptions are not kept,
Hath left me, and I desperate now approve
Desire is death, which physic did except.
Past cure I am, now reason is past care,
And frantic mad with evermore unrest.
My thoughts and my discourse as madmen's are,
At random from the truth vainly expressed;
  For I have sworn thee fair, and thought thee bright,
  Who are as black as hell, as dark as night.

Bruno's second sonnet quoted above shows in its form a striking concurrence with Shakespeare's Sonnet 126, in that each has only twelve lines, though the rhyme-scheme differs in each.[108] A further irregularity, frequent in Bruno's sonnets, occurs in Shakespeare's Sonnet 145, in which each line has one foot less than in other regularly composed sonnets.

After all that has been said, it seems to us impossible not to see the manifold connections between Shakespeare's works and the work of Giordano Bruno, and though we are far from maintaining that Shakespeare took Bruno as his definite model, or that Bruno exerted an overwhelming and lasting influence on him, there is scarcely any poet or writer among his contemporaries to whom we could attribute a greater influence on Shakespeare's formation. Naturally we do not question the broad influence on him of the English stage, as Shakespeare found it, and its productions. In all such investigations, too, it is hard to draw the line between the encouragement and stimulus that draws the younger writer into new paths or awakens new conceptions in him, and that which allows an already present similarity of outlook to emerge and arouses the younger writer's

---

[108] [Sonnet 126 is the last of the fair-youth sonnets: with the next poem, in a metaphorical sense, Shakespeare sets sail towards the dark lady. See how appropriate Bruno's own 12-line sonnet is to this development, especially in its final three lines.]

interest in his like-minded senior, without making him any different to what he would have been without the latter's example. Between these two types of intellectual influence there are so many intermediate degrees and so many imperceptible transitions that in an individual case it is scarcely possible to categorize such a relationship correctly and to draw a general conclusion from specific indices, especially when we have little or no solid information about the educational history of the person concerned. The individual's subjective judgement as to the originality or receptivity of the writer in question must be left to determine the degree of his dependence on a single model, and to come to a personal decision, as has been attempted here, concerning the demonstrable indices that reveal the intellectual affinity between the two, or the influence of the one on the other. It is certainly possible to demonstrate more of these traces in the works of Shakespeare and Bruno and to pursue them further than has been done here, and if the view of life disclosed in the works of these two were considered comprehensively by placing them side by side, much that was noteworthy in relation to the theme discussed here would emerge, but the dimensions of the inquiry could easily be so much enlarged that one might well wonder if the resulting findings, which must always fall short of certainty, would be proportionate to the labour of critical investigation. Yet in order not to injure Shakespeare or to arouse any misconceptions, the present inquiry cannot be concluded without noting an essential difference in the two men's outlook on life. By his doctrines Bruno assumed a position wholly outside Christianity, and many of his writings are hostile to it. He was not an atheist, though the accusation has sometimes been made; his faith finds expression, now in a kind of divine intoxication, now in a kind of pantheism, when he assumes the existence of an all-encompassing world-soul. In this whole domain Shakespeare shows not the slightest affinity with Bruno, and here too we come to the conclusion that Shakespeare kept his religious beliefs as distant as possible from his poetic representation. We thus find confirmed the view we have previously expressed, that his Christianity was as genuine and simple as we imagine his whole personality to have been.[109]

---

[109] Cf. *Shakespeare als Dichter*, pp. 120, 250; *Jahrbuch* 7, p. 191.

List of Primary Works Cited

Where the text is not identified here, the quotation is as cited originally by König.

Alexander, William, Earl of Stirling, *The Tragedy of Darius* [1603] (London, 1604; STC (2nd ed.) / 350)

Anacreontea, in *Greek Lyric, Volume 2: Anacreon, Anacreontea, Choral Lyric from Olympus to Alcman*. Edited and translated by David A. Campbell (Cambridge, MA, 1988)

Ariosto, Lodovico, *Satire*. Edited by Guido Davico Bonino (Milan, 1990)

Aristotle, *Physics, Volume I: Books 1-4*. Translated by P. H. Wicksteed, F. M. Cornford (Cambridge, MA, 1957)

Bruno, Giordano, *Dialoghi italiani*, 2 vols. Edited by Giovanni Gentile. Third edition by Giovanni Aquilecchia (Florence, 1958)

Calderon de la Barca, Pedro, *Life Is a Dream / La vida es sueño*. Edited and translated by Stanley Appelbaum (Mineola, NY, 2002)

Cervantes Saavedra, Miguel de, *The History of the Renowned Don Quixote de la Mancha*, 4 vols. Translated by several hands and published by Motteux (London, 1749)

Cicero, *On the Orator: Book 3. On Fate. Stoic Paradoxes. Divisions of Oratory*. Translated by H. Rackham (Cambridge, MA, 1942)

Cicero, *Pro Milone. In Pisonem. Pro Scauro. Pro Fonteio. Pro Rabirio Postumo. Pro Marcello. Pro*

Ligario. *Pro Rege Deiotaro*. Translated by N. H. Watts (Cambridge, MA, 1931)

D'Aubigné, Théodore Agrippa, *Les Aventures du baron de Faeneste*. Edited by Prosper Mérimée (Paris, 1855)

Goldoni, Carlo, *Il teatro comico*, in *Opere*. Edited by Gianfranco Folena (Milan, 1969)

Grazzini, Antonfrancesco, *La strega* (Venice, 1582)

Greene, Robert, *Friar Bacon and Friar Bungay* (London, 1594), STC (2nd ed.) / 12267

Jonson, Ben, *The Cambridge Edition of the Works of Ben Jonson* (Cambridge, 2014-)

[Macpherson, James] *The Poems of Ossian translated by James Macpherson, Esq.* (Leipzig, 1847)

Milton, John, *Paradise Lost*. Edited by Barbara K. Lewalski (Malden, MA, 2007)

Pindar, *Olympian Odes. Pythian Odes*. Edited and translated by William H. Race (Cambridge, MA, 1997)

Pulci, Luigi, *Morgante maggiore*. With a preface by Andrea Rubbi (Venice, 1784-1801)

Rabelais, François, *Œuvres de Rabelais*, 9 vols. Edited by M. Esmangart and Éloi Johanneau (Paris, 1823)

Rabelais, François, *Gargantua and Pantagruel*, 3 vols. Translated by Sir Thomas Urquhart (Books 1-3) and Peter Le Motteux (Books 4-5) (London, 1934)

Rabelais, François, *Pantagruel's Prognostication*. Translated by 'Democritus Pseudomantis' (London, 1660), EEBO-TCP, http://name.umdl.umich.edu/A57017.0001.001 [accessed 5 September 2023]

Seneca, *Moral Essays, Volume 3: De Beneficiis*. Translated by John W. Basore (Cambridge, MA, 1935)

Shakespeare, William, *The Norton Shakespeare*. Gen. ed. Stephen Greenblatt (New York, 1997)

Sophocles, *Ajax. Electra. Oedipus Tyrannus*. Edited and translated by Hugh Lloyd-Jones (Cambridge, MA, 1994)

Joannis Stobœi Florilegium, 4 vols. Edited by Thomas Gaisford (Oxford, 1822)

Tomkis, Thomas, *Albumazar* (London, 1615), STC (2nd ed.) / 24101

Verlato, Leonoro, *Rodopeia* (Venice, 1582)

Index of Shakespeare Passages Cited

Like the quotations in the text this index has been unified according to the 1997 edition of The Norton Shakespeare. Act, scene and line numbers are, therefore, as per that edition.

The figures in bold after the act, scene and line numbers refer to the chapters in which the passage in question is mentioned.

Plays

All's Well That Ends Well

1.1.37-39	**3**
1.2.20-21	**3**
2.3.1-5	**3**

Antony and Cleopatra

1.2.113-115	**3**

As You Like It

1.2.41-46	**3**
2.1.12-14	**3**
2.3.10-15	**3**
2.7.138	**1**
3.2.28	**3**
3.2.205-206	**1**
3.2.211	**3**
3.5.13	**3**

The Comedy of Errors

2.1.61-67   **3**

Coriolanus

1.1.117-129   **1**

Cymbeline

2.5.19-22   **3**

Hamlet

1.2.72-73	**3n**
1.2.129-130	**3**
1.2.146	**3**
1.4.16-18.4	**3**
1.4.18.11	**3**
[1.4.21-25	**1n**]
1.5.168	**3**
2.2.87-90	**1, 3**
2.2.91	**1**
2.2.111-112	**3**
2.2.185-186	**3**
2.2.191-195	**3**
2.2.244-245	**3**
2.2.251-255	**1n**
2.2.293-298	**2**
2.2.350-351	**3**
2.2.478	**3**
2.2.484	**3**
2.2.499-500	**3**

2.2.503-504	**2**
2.2.554-555	**3**
3.1.62-63	**1**
3.1.122-139	**3**
3.2.4-5	**2n**
3.2.18-25	**2**
3.2.61-62	**3**
3.2.126	**2**
3.2.127-130	**2**
3.2.180-181	**3**
3.4.59	**3**
4.3.21-31	**3**
4.3.33-34	**1**
4.4.23-29	**2**
4.7.95.3-95.5	**3**
5.1.187-195	**3**
5.2.102.31-32	**3**
5.2.158-161	**3**

1 Henry IV

1.2.21-26	**1**
3.3.4-9	**1**
3.3.79 s.d.	**1**
3.3.140-153	**1**
5.1.78	**1**

2 Henry IV

1.2.40	**1**
3.2.61-73	**1n**
4.3.54	**3**

Henry V

1.1.61   3
4.1.4-12   3

2 Henry VI (The First Part of the Contention)

4.2.149-150   2
4.7.24-27   2
4.9.5-13   1n

3 Henry VI (Richard Duke of York)

1.4.138   1

Henry VIII (All Is True)

1.1.141-145   3
1.2.112-119   3
2.2.21   3

Julius Caesar

1.2.53-60   3
3.1.76   2
5.5.72-74   3

King John

3.4.112-115   3
4.2.170   1

King Lear

1.2.12	**3**
1.2.99-106	**1**
3.2	**1**
3.4.97/98-100	**1n, 3**
4.1.2-6	**3**

Love's Labour's Lost

4.2.46-66	**3**
4.2.53-58	**3**
4.2.112-117	**3**
5.1	**3**
5.1.14	**3**
5.2.572-573	**1**

Macbeth

1.1.3	**1**
1.5.35-52	**3**
5.5.23	**1**

Measure for Measure

1.2.106-108	**3**
2.2.61-65	**2n**
3.1	**3**
3.1.14-15	**1n**
3.1.19-21	**3**
3.1.32-34	**1**

The Merchant of Venice

Dram. pers.	**1**
1.2.61-64	**2**
2.2.1-25	**3**
3.2.160-165	**2**
4.1.179-192	**1**
4.1.180	**2**
5.1.63-64	**2**
5.1.98	**3**
5.1.305-306	**1**

The Merry Wives of Windsor

5.5.12	**1**

Othello

1.1.118	**1**

Richard II

3.2.131-132	**3**
5.1.66-67	**3**
5.3.109-134	**2n**
5.5.60	**1**

Richard III

1.3.349-350	**2n**
3.4.96-101	**2**
4.2.117	**1**

Romeo and Juliet

1.1.169-174	3
1.3.44	1
1.4.58	3
2.2.8-26	3

The Tempest

1.1.25-29	1
1.1.41-43	1
1.1.52-54	1
2.1.143-168	1, 3n
4.1.148-158	1
4.1.156-157	3
5.1.33-57	1
5.1.220-221	1

Timon of Athens

3.7.89	1
4.3.418-421	1
4.3.428-437	1

Titus Andronicus

1.1.117-119	2(n)
2.3.192	1

Troilus and Cressida

1.3.94-124	1
3.3.90-97	3
3.3.98-106	3

3.3.113-118 **3**
3.3.139-144 **1**
5.3.109-110 **3n**

The Two Gentlemen of Verona
1.1.136-138 **1**
2.3   **3**
[2.3.15   **3n**]
4.4.17-19   **3**

Poems

The Phoenix and the Turtle
17   **1**

Sonnets
[All mentions are in chapter **3**]

45; 53; 59; 60; 71; 81; 89; 94; 126; 129; 137; 144; 145; 147; 148

Venus and Adonis
793-794   **2**

www.ingramcontent.com/pod-product-compliance
Lightning Source LLC
Chambersburg PA
CBHW030039100526
44590CB00011B/263